D1093015

THE MINISTRY
OF RECONCILIATION

THE MANDATE FOR
THE MINISTRY OF RECONCILIATION

Therefore, if any one is in Christ, he is a new creation; the old has passed away, behold, the new has come. All this is from God, who through Christ reconciled us to himself and gave us the ministry of reconciliation; that is, God was in Christ reconciling the world to himself, not counting their trespasses against them, and entrusting to us the message of reconciliation. So we are ambassadors for Christ, God making his appeal through us.—II Cor. 5:17-20a

THE MINISTRY
OF RECONCILIATION

GEORGIA HARKNESS

ABINGDON PRESS NASHVILLE
NEW YORK

1579273

CONTENTS

1. WHAT IS RECONCILIATION?

What is reconciliation? In these days of conflict and tension this is a term much bandied about, though often without a clear understanding of its meaning or foundations. It is bound to appear in most of the current church statements on social issues, always connoting something good and worthy of support by Christians. Indeed, if there is anything on which Christians of all varieties and intelligent secularists agree, it is that our current state of hostility and alienation is counterproductive, and that reconciliation is an imperative need in our present strife-torn, broken world.

Yet the foundations of reconciliation in Christian thought, and hence what it entails in Christian action, are too often left undefined. A number of the denominations have launched large-scale financial drives to secure funds for reconciliation. Granted that not one but many special projects need and merit support from such funds, but what is it that defines them as agencies of reconciliation?

Reconciliation is so broad a term that it can go off in numerous directions. On the other hand, it can be used too narrowly. A first task in this book will be to define the term. Then later we shall try to see what its biblical and theological foundations are and from these get some guidelines as to what must be done in today's world.

From a theological standpoint, the term reconciliation is often used—or at least it was formerly often used—to denote personal salvation through the atoning death of Christ. In consulting the Bible dictionaries and theological wordbooks on my shelves, I repeatedly find such observations as "see atonement; mediator; redemption; forgiveness; propitiation; wrath of God." In the older classic books on this subject—James Denney's *The Christian Doctrine of Reconciliation* (1917) and Vincent Taylor's *Forgiveness and Reconciliation* (1941)—the atoning death of Christ is precisely what it means. In consulting the library listings of contemporary books on reconciliation, one is struck with two findings: the paucity of such books in recent years, and the almost exclusively social emphasis given to the term. It is indicative of our times that we no longer hear much about atonement, nor do we equate it with reconciliation. In the volume of subject headings used in the catalogs of the Library of Congress, I find only two subheadings under "reconciliation." These are "peacemaking" and "quarreling"! Granted that these do bear a relation to reconciliation, even in the biblical and theological sense, it is apparent that reconciliation as atonement through Christ does not figure largely in contemporary thought.

Yet this is no reason to dismiss this connotation. As I hope to show in the next two chapters, this meaning has a very important place, both in the Bible and in the main stream of Christian theology up to recent years. Furthermore, if we look beneath the surface, it is intimately related to reconciliation in its vital social meaning, though we are under no obligation to conceive it in the same way that our forefathers have done.

A much more common understanding of reconciliation today is the bridging of rifts, sometimes between individuals in face-to-face and person-to-person relationships, but more

8

often between groups. Historians of the future will doubtless need to describe our era as one of deep divisions. There are rifts between and within political parties, between blacks and whites, between young people and their elders, between the well-to-do and the poor, between the conservative and radical in almost every field. The church is no exception, for while we have been drawn together ecumenically over the past sixty years with the Edinburgh International Missionary Conference of 1910 as a dateline in Protestantism and Vatican II in Roman Catholicism, there are still deep divisions within the denominations.

To no small degree, reconciliation is itself a bone of contention in the churches. It is not that reconciliation, when seen as denoting something very good and desirable, is repudiated. Like "motherhood" and "fatherland," the word calls up an agreeable feeling—until one begins to shape his actions by what he understands it to mean. To some it means reconciliation to God through the atoning death of Christ, and hence the exalting and proclaiming of a gospel of personal salvation in which politics and social action through the churches have no place. To others it means getting out "where the action is" and engaging in projects, endeavors, and demonstrations of power to enable those long deprived of their just rights to come to their full dignity as persons. To those of the second opinion, the church is likely to seem actuated by a "theology of rift" because of its long neglect of the needs of the world, while to those of the first opinion, the social actionists are not reconcilers, but troublemakers.

Though the reconciliation of person to person and group to group is a valid and very much needed form of reconciliation, Christian guidelines still are needed. When, if ever, does the use of force in behalf of justice find a legitimate place in Christian ethics? At what point does conciliation—

the placating of an enemy without convincing him—replace reconciliation? How shall we avoid the twin evils of appeasement on the one hand and paternalism on the other? The author makes no promise of giving a final answer to these recurrent questions, but we shall at least look at them seriously.

A common synonym of reconciliation is peacemaking, and it is not surprising that the Library of Congress listings make this affiliation. Furthermore, we are told on the highest Christian authority, "Blessed are the peacemakers, for they shall be called sons of God." In the sense of the biblical *shalom,* this comes as near as any other term to stating its meaning. Eugene C. Bianchi in his excellent book, *Reconciliation—the Function of the Church,*[1] adopts *shalom* as the goal toward which the church should work if it is to move away from dualism and the consequent theology of rift which are its legacy from the Augustinian Platonism and the Aristotelian-Thomistic tradition of the long past. Of these he says:

These Western traditions, affecting and being influenced by the societal forms of Constantinianism and feudalism in the church, have left us with an inadequately dualistic approach to the church's place in the world. The theology of rift is a negative dimension of the cleavages inherent in much of this thinking of the past. It has affected our thinking about body and soul, sex and sanctity, nature and supernature, heaven and earth, church and world.[2]

Shalom, however, is a term which describes men's living at peace with nature, with themselves, with their neighbors, and with God. In this inclusive sense, it is indeed very close to the meaning of reconciliation. But note that it must be thought of in this inclusive sense. Peace as the absence

10

of conflict is not reconciliation. The avoidance of issues in order to keep the peace can become a step toward the antithesis of reconciliation.

To many readers, doubtless the most familiar use of the term we are endeavoring to define is found in the name of the Fellowship of Reconciliation. This is a Christian pacifist organization which was founded in 1915 during the first world war, and which has persisted not only to the present but has become much stronger in these recent war-torn years. This is a reconciling agency which, though small in numbers, has exerted an important constructive influence throughout the years. Yet Christian conscientious objection, whether with regard to all wars or a particular war, is only one approach to the complex problems of peace in our time. It is a witness to be taken seriously, but both the Christian gospel and the nature of our world require the ministry of reconciliation to take many forms.

What, then, is reconciliation? The foregoing observations have revealed the difficulty of arriving at a definition which is neither too broad nor too narrow, too vague nor too limiting. I shall not pretend to have overcome all these pitfalls. Yet I will hazard a definition, as the term will be used in this book. To fill in its content will be the aim of the ensuing chapters.

Reconciliation is the overcoming of alienation, estrangement, hostility, and enmity through the spirit, and it is the resulting acts of friendliness, understanding, and good will. Thus far, in a general sense reconciliation need not be distinctively Christian. It can take place through the attitudes and acts of Christians, of those of other religious faiths, or of those of no faith except a trust in the possibility of reconciliation rooted in a minimal trust in human nature.

When reconciliation becomes Christian reconciliation, it

11

is that which is felt and done in the spirit of Christ. Since the spirit of the sinless Christ has no complete replica in sinful humanity, it might be more accurate to say that in Christian reconciliation, one aims sincerely, conscientiously, and with the best wisdom available to him to act in the spirit of Christ. He does this trusting in God's guidance and support, as Christ himself did, and goes ahead into whatever may be required of him with courage and confidence.

The ministry of reconciliation, of which Paul speaks so movingly in II Corinthians 5: 18-20 (which gives the title, and I trust, the keynote of this book) is very closely related to the love of which Paul writes immortal words in I Corinthians 13. Nevertheless, there is a shade of difference and an important one, not so much in the quality as in the occasion. One is called to love at all times, amid smooth places or rough, in happy times or sad, in the presence of friend or foe. To do this is not easy, and one must overcome a self-centered reluctance—in this sense, be reconciled inwardly. But when we speak of reconciliation, there are outward barriers also to be overcome. Reconciliation always implies a prior negative condition. One may feel the barrier is between him and God, or him and his neighbor, or one may feel it exists within a particular group or in the total world around him. But there must be some barrier, outward and usually inward also—though this may be unrecognized—or there would be no need of reconciliation.

Thus we may say that reconciliation is *agape* in action, but *agape* felt and expressed in the face of all that stands in the way of its fulfillment. It is not something to be engaged in by soft and flabby souls, any more than it can be by stern and callous ones, though an inner reconciliation may be the answer to both these extremes. Amid the frustrating realities of the human situation, love that is truly Christian "bears all things, believes all things, hopes all things, endures all things," and thus becomes a reconciling force to be used by God in the advancement of his long purposes.

We noted a moment ago that *shalom,* or "peace" in the biblical sense, is also a very close synonym of reconciliation. This is true as an ingredient of the spirit that prompts one to act in reconciling love. Yet it is also the fruit of reconciling love. It is the high reward of one who does not seek the peace of passivity through avoidance of struggle, but who sees his duty and does it in trust of God and the power of love.

There is need of reconciliation at all times with oneself, his neighbor, and that object of ultimate concern and devotion which one regards as his God. This is felt in the spiritual yearnings of mankind, however dimly but persistently, and it is being felt today. In view of the present lack of political, economic, racial, family, or cultural unity which prevails, it is not surprising that the need of reconciliation of group to group stands out most vividly. The need of the overcoming of hostility and enmity between groups is overwhelming, but it is not likely to take place in any deep or lasting fashion unless individuals have their values geared in the direction of friendship, understanding, and goodwill.

While Christian faith and love are not the only sources of a redirection of values which can lead to reconciliation, they are vital and hence important sources. It is the evidence of a long history that when Christian faith and love are experienced in depth, as they too seldom are, they are the most potent sources for the overcoming of alienation and estrangement, hostility and enmity between and within individuals. Will they work in group relations? It depends upon the action which they motivate. Granted there is truth in Reinhold Niebuhr's thesis about "moral man and immoral society" [3] and the need of power for the establishment of social justice, it still remains true that much depends on the tenor of spirit, and hence of action, among leaders and in a democracy among those led. With a wide-enough base of persons in whom Christian faith and love are joined with political discernment and insight, social hope could be much nearer to fulfillment than it now seems to be.

These are very complex times, and nothing is gained by oversimplifying them. There is a war which drags on its weary way, and which seems to vast numbers of Americans, younger and older alike, to have been a gross mistake at best and a colossal injustice at worst. There is a black people who have suffered centuries of oppression and injustice, and are now demanding—and at times overdemanding—recognition of their self-identity and just rights. There are great numbers of the poor, and even of the hungry, in America who are content no longer to live in ghettos and rural shacks while affluent America engages in "conspicuous consumption." There is a whole generation of the young—students, hippies and just ordinary young people—who, in protest against a materialistic and *status quo* culture, react against the Establishment. And as they do so, many flout the basic sexual standards of the ages and seek a quasi-mystical illumination through drugs. In such a situation, what contribution can be expected of Christian faith and love?

A great deal, if Christian faith and love motivate action consistent with their essential natures. Such action requires a sound theological base as well as good intentions. In much of today's protest against the so-called "irrelevance" of the churches, this base is weak or lacking. Love, indeed, is projected as the motive of service to the victims of social injustice, but often in a quite unloving spirit toward those who also for years have been concerned about social justice, but who have chosen other modes of action. The love commandment of Jesus is advocated without reference to, and sometimes in denial of, the God of Jesus, and thus a transcendent base of faith and hope are eliminated.

It would be too serious a charge to claim that the shifts in recent years toward a secularized theology have caused the social evils of our time. These have many complex causes, and concern for the secular world is a much-needed move in quarters where it was previously absent. Yet lack of a firm God-centered, Christ-centered base in its manifold points of outreach to human life has certainly weakened an otherwise constructive thrust. I have not seen this better stated than in the words of John Bennett:

A stripped-down, relevant version of Christianity may be effective for the moment in dealing with a particular problem, but it provides little guidance for the complexities opened up by that very problem. It fails to mediate the grace of forgiveness and of new life that the whole person needs, and it knows little of the sources of reconciliation that society requires for its healing.[4]

Whatever political or economic channels may be used for the healing of society—and those needing to be used are many—it is essential that spirit and action converge. However right the action in terms of changing structures, performing helpful acts, or supplying the funds to finance them, "the gift without the giver is bare" unless a genuine friendliness, good will, and concern for the persons being served form the motivation of what is done. Furthermore, though complete understanding of another's situation in the social structure—to say nothing of his soul—may not be humanly possible, lack of such understanding is a basic reason why condescension, paternalism, and "tokenism" are distasteful barriers to reconciliation in human relations.

Complete understanding obviously calls for knowledge and the use of one's mind. But it is also mediated through the Christ-spirit in a human personality, and most of us know humble souls in whom this spirit has shone forth to a remarkable degree. This is essential to the quality of reconciling love. Yet we cannot proceed from this affirmation to the declaration that the Christ-spirit is all we need, or we may end in a pious inactivity, enjoying our religion and not doing much about it, which is not really in Christ's spirit at all. I recall that one of my earliest pieces of writing was prompted by hearing it affirmed in unctuous tones, "All the world needs is the spirit of Jesus." Doubtless it is such statements, unsupported by action, which have led the critics to say that the churches have preached love for centuries without practicing it.

I do not believe this charge to be true, though there is enough truth in it that it ought to stir us into action. Perhaps we may call it a half-truth, though a quarter-truth—if there is such a thing—might be nearer the right proportion. In any case, it is nearer the truth to say that the Christian church, as the carrier of Christian faith and love, has through the centuries been the primary agent of reconciliation. In this task, the Christian church has again and again been used by God for the reconciliation not only of man to God and of man to himself, but of man to man through its services to those in many forms of need. It is with the hope of its doing more through a clearer understanding of a Christian ministry of reconciliation that this book is being undertaken.

The foregoing pages have, I trust, indicated to the reader what the author understands reconciliation to be and to require of those who would be carriers of the message entrusted to us, as "ambassadors of Christ, making his appeal through us." But how then shall we proceed within this book?

The next two chapters will include a survey of what the Bible has to say about reconciliation, both in the Old and New Testaments. There need be no apology for beginning with a biblical base, for while the Bible does not contain all the world's wisdom, it is the chief cornerstone of Christian faith and morals, not in its situation-conditioned aspects, but in its disclosure of universal and lasting truth. During this survey, we shall give considerable attention to reconciliation as atonement, and shall hope to show both that man's reconciliation to God is relevant to today's world, and that the Bible has other things to say about reconciliation which we disregard at our peril.

We shall then turn to the contemporary scene. The problem of "man against himself" and what contemporary understandings of human nature can tell us must be looked at, for as alienation and estrangement infect the human soul and cry out for reconciliation, so also do we find within the human psyche the potential which makes reconciliation possible.

But what of social disharmony? Since the tensions and conflicts of group relations loom up as the largest problem of our living together on this planet, we cannot bypass them. Since they are so enormous, any discussion of them must be kept within sober and restricted limits. Yet to omit them would be to retreat to the proverbial ivory tower.

Because of this need, two chapters are devoted to reconciliation in group relations. The first of these centers on the small group, or person-to-person relations. Here, the keynote is friendship. Since heretofore comparatively little has been done in the way of a serious analysis of what friendship is and its place in social ethics, the chapter begins with this consideration. It is followed by some observations on this basis in three major problems of small group relations: marriage and the family, the generation gap, and harmony within the church.

Yet our most divisive and difficult problems are in the area of large group relations. What reconciliation can we expect to achieve when great numbers of people are pitted against each other, with a "dividing wall of hostility" between them? Here the primary answer lies in justice. So, though justice, unlike friendship, has been analyzed many times, the author ventures to say what she believes it to be and to require. On this foundation, discussions are then presented of three other contemporary social issues: race and black power, the women's liberation movement, and crime and its punishment.

These issues to which particular attention is given by no means cover the whole gamut of areas in which reconciliation is sorely needed in today's world. But the book must stop somewhere, and the reader can perhaps discern from what is said on these matters the direction in which the author believes we should move.

The concluding chapter takes up a matter crucial to all the rest—the strategy of the Christian in controversy. Here the main directives stem from the Bible, and in particular from certain injunctions of Paul which have universal and ageless relevance. From here on, let the reader take the problems and their solutions where he will!

Along the way, some observations will be offered as to the ministry of reconciliation through the churches, though I have not intended to restrict what is said to this field. I do not despair of the churches as some do, for I believe that they are now doing, and will continue to do, significant things in the service of human need. Yet more and better things must be done. So let us get on with them!

2. RECONCILIATION
IN THE OLD TESTAMENT

In contemporary discussions of reconciliation, the emphasis is commonly laid on the reconciliation of person to person, whether in immediate or group relations, and such references to the Bible as emerge are assumed to be covered by the injunction to love one's neighbor. This, indeed, is basic; yet the second of the two great commandments requires the first for its fullest meaning.

Reconciliation involves more than love of neighbor; it includes reconciliation with God, with one's own inner self, and with the total world of nature and humanity insofar as these impinge upon us. In both the Old and the New Testaments, the need of reconciliation in all of these senses is a major theme. While the word is used in relatively few instances, what it stands for appears repeatedly.

We shall begin with some word study, which may suggest some new meanings of familiar but often discarded terms. Then we shall trace the theme of man's reconciliation with God, which includes his reconciliation with himself and his world, through its stages of development from primitive myth through the law codes to the high insights in the words of the prophets and sages. Then in another section, we shall follow the same sequence in relation to the reconciliation of man to man and group to group. They intertwine and impinge on each other, yet the vertical and the horizontal aspects of reconciliation are not identical.

Some word study

My concordance of the King James Version lists the noun "reconciliation" or some form of the verb "to reconcile" eight times in the Old Testament against twelve in the New. Yet when one compares these passages with the corresponding ones in the Revised Standard Version, some rather surprising results appear. In the Old Testament, the term is translated "to atone" or "to make atonement for" in all but one instance. This exception is in I Samuel 29:4, where the context makes it clear that the reconciliation is on the person-to-person level. Yet in the New Testament the proportions are reversed, and the term is retained as reconciliation in all but one passage, where it is rendered as "expiation." These terms, "atonement" and "expiation," call for some attention.

The English word "atone" is derived from the phrase "at one." This is not a play on words, as is sometimes suggested, but an actual derivation. For evidence, consult your dictionary! Atonement in its original sense means "at-one-ment," or "to be in a harmonious relation with." This is very close to being a synonym for reconciliation. The term in customary theological usage has taken on the more restricted meaning of the act or process by which man's estrangement from God is overcome. A Christian doctrine of atonement centers on the work of Christ, and especially the death of Christ, for man's redemption. Yet atonement appears repeatedly in the Old Testament, not only in those passages where the King James Version renders it as reconciliation, but in many others.

To anticipate our New Testament studies, another fact

appears surprising, that is, in view of the long-standing centrality of atonement in Christian theology. Only once does the word "atonement" appear in the King James Version of the New Testament, in Romans 5:11, and in RSV this is replaced by "reconciliation." Furthermore, "propitiation," so often associated with atonement as making satisfaction to God in his wrath, appears not once in the Old Testament. The King James has it three times in the New Testament—Romans 3:25, I John 2:2, and I John 4:10— but in each instance the RSV renders it "expiation."

But does not "expiation" mean "propitiation"? I find this important distinction in the Abingdon *Interpreter's Dictionary of the Bible*:

The word "propitiation" suggests that God, alienated by man's sin, requires something to appease his anger before he will again show favor to the sinner. "Expiation" recognizes that a hindrance to right relations has been created by the sin, and that this is removed by the means of atonement, but it does not locate the hindrance in God.[1]

What is the significance of these words for our examination of reconciliation in the Bible? The literalists and traditionalists are likely to say, as they often have, that the translators of the Revised Standard Version have fixed up the words to suit their own theology! This is far from being the case. What emerges from these studies is that the propitiation of the wrath of an angry God who must be appeased by the death of a sacrificial victim is not the basic biblical understanding of atonement. Furthermore, atonement in the fullest New Testament sense is reconciliation, the removal of barriers between man and God which man by his sin and indifference to the divine demands has brought upon himself. In short, it is not God, but man, who needs to be reconciled.

The reconciliation of man to God

We are ready now to observe how these developments appear in the Old Testament. First, it must be said that the wrath of God does appear in the Old Testament, sometimes in apparently vindictive and certainly in startling terms, and often without a very clear distinction as to whether it is the sin or the sinner against which, or against whom, this wrath is directed. Yet one cannot read the Old Testament in proper perspective without recognizing that the God of the Covenant, who loved Israel enough to make its people his chosen people, never stopped loving his wayward and often unfaithful people. It is sometimes said that judgment is the primary note in the Old Testament, with the love of God appearing only in a few great passages like Hosea 11:1-4. It is truer to say that judgment and love are so mingled that even God's righteous indignation, his terrible condemnation of sin, stems from moral demands which are the fruit of his love. In this context God's anger does not need to be appeased, but the people's alienation through infidelity must be overcome.

In the primitive, mythico-poetic, but very meaningful stories of the early chapters in Genesis, this begins to be very evident. Adam and Eve are driven out of their idyllic garden, not because the knowledge of good and evil is in itself a bad thing but because they desired in their human presumption to be "like God." Presently, both economic and familial strife breaks out as Abel the shepherd is killed by his brother Cain, a tiller of the soil. Numerous generations pass, until "the Lord saw that the wickedness of man was great in the earth." An anthropomorphic deity is so dismayed that he considers blotting out man and every other living thing from the earth, but he does not do it. Noah and the ark are God's answer. As the dove returns to

22

give a harbinger of hope, God establishes the covenant of the rainbow, promises that "while the earth remains, seed-time and harvest, cold and heat, summer and winter, day and night shall not cease," and again gives the commission to man, made in his own image, to be fruitful and multiply and bring forth abundantly on the earth.

In these stories, reconciliation shines through God's displeasure at man's sin. Yet the story which most graphically portrays the disharmony upon earth is that of the Tower of Babel. Here again, human presumption is its own undoing, and those who are meant to be one people with a common language are scattered over the face of the earth with a great confusion of tongues. It need scarcely be added that the reunion had not occurred at the time the story was written, nor has it yet.

We must glance now at some of the ritualistic forms of atonement, or reconciliation, as a deeper consciousness of sin and the need to make amends for it developed. There are numerous references to priestly acts whereby offerings of the blood of bulls or goats are specified "to make atonement in the holy place" (Lev. 6: 30) or "to make atonement for all Israel" (II Chron. 29: 24). In some of the passages, notably Leviticus 8: 15 and Leviticus 16: 18, 20, atonement must be made *for* the altar as well as *on* it. Ezekiel at a later point speaks of making atonement for the temple (45: 20). Apparently a breach of the Covenant was so serious that it defiled not only the people but their sacred shrine, and sin offerings must be made if reconciliation with God was to be had.

In addition to the offerings of the blood of slain animals, we find also in Leviticus 16: 20-22 the curious provision that Aaron should take a live goat, confess the sins of the people and place them upon its head, and send it into the wilderness to bear away their sins. From this we have the term "scapegoat" in the English language. Furthermore, it had its influence in later centuries in the development of a substitutionary theory of the atonement whereby Christ bears the brunt of our human sin. Of this we shall say more in the next chapter.

If the idea that sin can be forgiven and alienation removed by animal sacrifices seems crude and primitive, as it must, it is well to remember that sin to the Hebrew mind was a serious matter. There is scarcely a page of the Old Testament which does not have some reference to sin, whether as missing the mark, or as an unconscious wandering from the right way, or deliberate rebellion against God. It is in lack of fidelity to the Covenant that the basic sin resides, but this takes many forms of infraction of God's holy will.

Moral responsibility is everywhere presupposed. Yet it is also recognized that sinful acts may be done through error or ignorance, with a differentiation in the penalty. Among the provisions for blood or burnt or cereal offerings, a distinction is drawn between "the person who commits an error, when he sins unwittingly" and "the person who does anything with a high hand," the former to be forgiven when the priest has made atonement and the latter to be cut off from among his people. (Num. 15:27-31)

Those were days of an emerging moral consciousness, deeply intertwined with religious conviction. The ritualistic offerings on behalf of reconciliation with Yahweh were not all that was required for compassionate service to the needy, as the social prophets were soon to point out. Yet they did serve to keep alive a sense of obligation to their God, and this was of no small importance. In the book of Judges, filled as it is with wars and apostasies, we nevertheless find Gideon building an altar to the Lord and calling it, "The Lord is peace." (6:24)

The religious consciousness of the Hebrew people was

destined to rise above blood and burnt offerings to the for-giveness by God of those who truly repent of their sins, and the call to penitence is sounded again and again. This higher note of reconciliation through man's penitence and God's lovingkindness, or steadfast love as the Revised Stan-dard Version has it, appears clearly in the Psalms. These passages are difficult to date since this "hymnbook of the second temple" contains poetry written all the way from the tenth century B.C. to the second. Yet it is clear that in these majestic outpourings of the human spirit, it is not ritualistic offerings but an inner commitment of soul that matters. A few examples must suffice:

> Remember not the sins of my youth, or my transgressions;
>> according to thy steadfast love remember me,
>> for thy goodness' sake, O Lord! (25:7)

> Have mercy on me, God, according to thy steadfast love;
>> according to thy abundant mercy blot out my transgres-sions.
> Wash me thoroughly from my iniquity,
>> and cleanse me from my sin. (51:1)

> If thou, O lord, shouldst mark iniquities,
>> Lord, who could stand?
> But there is forgiveness with thee,
>> that thou mayest be feared. (130:3)

So also is sounded the note of resolute security in God:

> For God alone my soul waits in silence;
>> from him comes my salvation.
> He only is my rock and my salvation,
>> my fortress; I shall not be greatly moved. (62:1)

And since peace, the biblical *shalom,* is such close kin to reconciliation, this note, also in the Psalms, should not be overlooked:

Let me hear what God the Lord will speak,
   for he will speak peace to his people,
     to his saints, to those who turn to him in their hearts. . . .

Steadfast love and faithfulness will meet;
   righteousness and peace will kiss each other.
Faithfulness will spring up from the ground,
   and righteousness will look down from the sky. (85:8-11)

Such words as these have been known and loved through the centuries and repeated times without number in services of both Hebrew and Christian worship. This is sufficient evidence that they strike to the heart of the human predicament and offer the most vivifying kind of reconciliation. While they continue to comfort and to challenge, the directives regarding ritualistic purification are passed over as relics of primitivism.

Yet it is in the words of the major prophets that the repudiation of reconciliation with God through external agencies becomes most explicit. With variations according to each man's temperament and his times, the prophets rang the changes insistently on four major themes: supreme allegiance to Yahweh, economic justice for all, the placing of righteousness above ritualistic correctness, and the inevitable doom which a loving but just God must send on the unrepentant.

Some of the most familiar words of the Old Testament are those in which these notes are sounded. One who is familiar with its wider sweep can hardly fail to note the contrast between earlier ritualistic prescriptions and the words of Amos as he speaks for God:

I hate, I despise your feasts,
   and I take no delight in your solemn assemblies.
Even though you offer me your burnt offerings and
    cereal offerings,
   I will not accept them,

26

and the peace offerings of your fatted beasts
I will not look upon. (5: 21-22)

A contrast is often drawn between Amos' plea for social
justice and Hosea's proclamation of God's love. There is a
difference in emphasis at these points; yet in their repudiation of sin offerings as an agency of reconciliation, they are
at one. It could not be put more bluntly than in the words
of Hosea as he, too, speaks in the name of God:

For I desire steadfast love and not sacrifice,
the knowledge of God, rather than burnt offerings. (6: 6)

Isaiah was as stern as Amos in his denunciation of cere-
monialism as a substitute for human kindness, as gentle as
Hosea in portraying God's forgiving love. For a majestic
portrayal of his conception of Yahweh's moral demands
and proffered salvation we may look to Isaiah 1: 14-20,
though this note appears repeatedly in his message. Micah
announces the human costs of reconciliation in requirements far more exacting than burnt offerings in the great
familiar words of Micah 6: 6-8.

While the older covenant between Yahweh and his people
is never lost sight of, Jeremiah's testimony to a new covenant written in the hearts of men (31: 31-34) points to a
higher form of reconciliation with God. It is one of the
high watermarks of the Old Testament. Second Isaiah also
abounds in great passages about God's deliverance, not only
from sin, but from fear and inner alienation. To a degree
not found elsewhere he links together the thought of God
as creator and redeemer, particularly in the majestic sweep
of chapter 40. The power of God and the love of God are
indissolubly connected, as in 54: 4-5, to banish fear and a
sense of separation. However the Suffering Servant of
Isaiah 53 is to be understood, this portrays unmistakably a

reconciliation with God through redemptive suffering, which is far removed from ritualistic purification through the blood of bulls and goats.

The passages from the prophets, thus briefly surveyed, are among the greatest, and hence the most familiar, in the Old Testament. They have been quoted time and again as a call to social action by the churches. This is good; they merit being quoted. Yet in the way they are often used today, I am uneasy at some points. First, the Old Testament rituals of purification were not all bad; they held the people together, were a reminder of their covenant, and afforded a much-needed sense of reconciliation and forgiveness. Second, to equate the contemporary services of worship in our churches with ancient purification rites and to speak of "the noise of solemn assemblies" in contrast with needed social action is to set up a false antithesis. The church exists both to comfort and to challenge, and the need to do more challenging of social evils does not detract from its need to comfort, restore, and build up the inner life. Third, not all of those who are most vocal in condemning the church for its futility and calling it to action manifest the steadfast faith in God which is found in psalmist and prophet. Without such a faith, there is nothing distinctive in the message of the church, and nothing to carry it through the long, dark days of the struggle with evil in our time.

The reconciliation of man to man

To turn from these high messages of the prophets with their summons to social justice to the daily pursuits of the Hebrews in their man-to-man and group-to-group relations is something of a "come-down," for one has to look hard to find much evidence of reconciliation in them. Much of the Old Testament deals with battles, conquests and counter-conquests, intrigue and cruelty. The belligerence of the people as they seek to assert power over their enemies is projected onto their God, and Yahweh becomes a God of battles, fighting for his chosen people against their foes.

Nevertheless, there are many words about peace in the Old Testament, not only in the Messianic prophecies of the coming of the Prince of Peace, but much earlier. Let it be remembered that, even to the present when all men yearn for peace, wars continue to be fought in which divine sanction is claimed for "our side" as the war is pursued with a sense of high moral duty.

The reconciliation of man to man and of group to group in the Old Testament can principally be found in three types of literature: the narratives of reconciliation between individuals, the provisions of the law codes, and again the words spoken by the prophets and sages. Let us note some examples.

As for the narratives, there is the interesting story of the reconciliation of Jacob and Esau in Genesis 32 and 33, though it is a bit difficult to judge whether the reconciliation between the brothers is due to brotherly love or to astute strategy. Esau seems to come out as still the more magnanimous of the two. There is the lovely story in I Samuel 24 of David's sparing Saul's life in the cave of the wilderness of Engedi, and the reconciliation which follows Saul's discovery of this act of magnanimity. In David's quarrel with his son Absalom there is a touching note in his instruction to his leaders, "Deal gently for my sake with the young man Absalom" (II Sam. 18:5), and still greater poignancy in his lament at the news of Absalom's death. (II Sam. 18:31-33) Not only is there fine drama in such stories which make them appealing, but they light up the social picture in a dark time.

In looking at group relations as they are reflected in the law codes of Israel, several considerations must be kept in mind. In the first place they reflect a standard of conduct higher than was commonly practiced, as is seen from the historical narratives. This is not surprising, for it is virtually always the case, and is true in the U.S.A. of today's world. A more distinctive consideration is that the religion of the Hebrews was very much of an everyday, down-to-earth, even "worldly" affair. Yahweh could be found at the altar or in the temple, "high and lifted up," as Isaiah found him (Is. 6:1), but he was also present in field and home, in marketplace and battleground. The created world was not itself divinized, as in some Oriental religions, but it was God's world in which man was bidden to "be fruitful and multiply" and to "subdue the earth" under the Lord's all-seeing eye.

This conviction merged with the ordinary forces of social change to give a distinctive tone to Israel's moral code as embodied in the laws prescribed for group relations. On the one hand, there were borrowings from the neighboring peoples and the natural adaptations of a predominantly agricultural society which was emerging into nationhood. At the same time, as the codes were formulated, it was the conviction of the Hebrew people that "God spoke all these words, saying. . . ." (Exod. 20:1)

The result was the Ten Commandments, of such universal relevance and depth of insight that they still are an important guide to human behavior. The provisions of the second Table of the Law, "You shall not kill, . . . commit adultery, . . . steal, . . . bear false witness, . . . covet." . . . show an amazing discernment as to the importance of protecting human life, the family, property rights, social integrity, and all that the individual has a right to call his own. The other three major codifications of Hebrew law, the Covenant Code, the Deuteronomic Code and the Holiness Code, are more situation-oriented, but nevertheless contain many provisions reflecting an advanced moral insight. A few examples must suffice.[2]

In spite of blood revenge and the *lex talionis* ("an eye for an eye and a tooth for a tooth"), cities of refuge were provided to which one who had slain another unintentionally might go to find protection. (Num. 35:6-34; Deut. 19:1-13; Josh. 20:1-9) The distinction between premeditated and accidental injury is stressed repeatedly in Hebrew law and with it the beginnings of a transcending of Jewish exclusiveness. The difference between highhanded crime and offenses done through error or ignorance applies equally to the people of Israel and to the stranger who sojourns with them. (Num. 15:29-30) The "stranger that is within the gates," like the Hebrew and his servants, is to be given a day of rest one day in seven. (Exod. 20:10; Deut. 5:14)

One was forbidden to wrong or oppress a stranger in recollection that the Hebrews, too, had been strangers in the land of Egypt. (Exod. 22:21) Quite explicit provisions were given for the protection of Hebrew slaves under various circumstances. (Exod. 21:2-11, 16, 20-21, 26-27) Widows and orphans were not to be afflicted. (Exod. 22:22-24) Property rights were guarded in injuctions not only against stealing but against negligence in the care of one's cattle (Exod. 21:28-34). A high degree of magnanimity is presupposed in the requirement that if one finds his enemy's ox or ass gone astray and caught under its pack, instead of leaving it there he must do all he can to restore it to its owner. (Exod. 23:4-5) One wonders how often this was lived up to!

These provisions of the Covenant Code are generally dated from the early days of the occupancy of Canaan. Thus they had not been influenced by the great prophets of social justice. There are striking resemblances between

31

many of these provisions and the Code of Hammurabi, probably not directly borrowed, but influenced by a common fund of legal tradition in the Fertile Crescent. Yet they were part of the *Covenant* Code, and the Covenant gave to Hebrew law both a high ethical impulse and a religious fervor that transcended the outlook of the surrounding peoples.

These provisions may seem to have more to do with social justice than with reconciliation. Yet justice is a very vital ingredient of a society where reconciliation can prevail. It always has been, and still is, with hostility and strife bound to emerge in its absence.

The greatest Hebrew word on the reconciliation of man to man was to appear later in the Holiness Code, which was probably compiled after the return from exile. Its recurring theme is the exhortation to Israel to be holy even as Yahweh is holy. Its high point is in Leviticus 19:17-18:

You shall not hate your brother in your heart, but you shall reason with your neighbor, lest you bear sin because of him. You shall not take vengeance or bear any grudge against the sons of your own people, but you shall love your neighbor as yourself: I am the Lord.

Glance at the surrounding items, and one finds a strange mixture of earlier ethical insights, temple ritual, and the minutiae of Jewish law. It is an enduring miracle that Jesus selected it from all the lore of the Old Testament to give it the immortal place which it holds today, and doubtless will hold to the end of time.

Turning from the legal to the wisdom literature of the Old Testament, one finds in the book of Proverbs many homey and down-to-earth bits of counsel, more than a few of which point to the avoidance of strife. For example,

A soft answer turns away wrath,
  but a harsh word stirs up anger. (15:1)

The beginning of strife is like letting out water;
  so quit before the quarrel breaks out. (17:14)

Drive out a scoffer, and strife will go out,
  and quarreling and abuse will cease. (22:10)

It is better to live in a desert land
  than with a contentious and fretful woman. (21:19)

Such passages indicate a prudential wisdom born of an observation of human nature and its reaction to circumstances. There is nothing specifically religious about them. Yet at one point the author rises to such greatness that Paul quotes his words:

If your enemy is hungry, give him bread to eat;
  and if he is thirsty, give him water to drink;
for you will heap coals of fire on his head,
  and the Lord will reward you. (25:21-22; cf. Rom. 12:20)

Paul does well to add the words, "Do not be overcome by evil, but overcome evil with good." It must sadly be observed that the moral consciousness of Christendom has not yet risen to the point where there is a general willingness to obey this injunction.

It was noted earlier that peace, or *shalom*, is a term used many times in the Old Testament, and that it is both an ingredient and a fruit of reconciliation. The term is used for peace within the soul, between individuals, and among nations. Such passages are found not only in the Psalms and words of the prophets but in the early historical literature as well. There are too many of these to cite in full.

Let the reader consult his concordance! But a few uses of the term may be mentioned.

The salutation, "Peace be with you!" used by Jesus in his resurrection appearances, and still a meaningful greeting to both Jews and Christians, is found repeatedly in the Old Testament. (Jud. 6:23; 19:20; I Sam. 25:6; I Chron. 12:18; Ps. 122:8; Dan. 4:1) Peace is bestowed by God and is to be prayed for. (Lev. 26:6; Num. 6:26; I Kgs. 2:33; II Kgs. 20:19; Ps. 122:6-7; Prov. 16:7; Jer. 29:7) There is no peace for the wicked (Isa. 48:22; 57:21); yet secure in God's care and in moral rectitude, one may dwell in peace. (Ps. 4:8; 34:14; 37:37; 85:8; Isa. 26:3) A beautiful picture of the peaceable habitation of the future is found in the words of Isaiah:

> Then justice will dwell in the wilderness,
>   and righteousness abide in the fruitful field.
> And the effect of righteousness will be peace,
>   and the result of righteousness, quietness and trust
>   for ever.
> My people will abide in a peaceful habitation,
>   in secure dwellings, and in quiet resting places. (32: 16-18)

Yet the greatest word in the Old Testament—and perhaps in any literature—on the conquest of war and the establishment of reconciliation on a national, and today we would need to say on a global, scale is found elsewhere in Isaiah, in chapter 2:2-4. It is too familiar to require quotation. It is restated by Micah in chapter 4:1-3. Micah may have been a disciple of Isaiah, and in any case he paid this passage the tribute of seeing its beauty and power. Then he rounds off the passage to a full crescendo, after the promise that "nation shall not lift up sword against nation, neither shall they learn war any more," with these words:

but they shall sit every man under his vine and under his fig
    tree,
  and none shall make them afraid;
  for the mouth of the Lord of hosts has spoken. (4:4)

He has, indeed! But when shall the nations give heed?
  With this magnificent prophecy to guide us toward the future, we bring to a close this survey of reconciliation as the Old Testament writers conceived it. Let us turn now to the New Testament.

1579273

3. RECONCILIATION
IN THE NEW TESTAMENT

In the New Testament we shall find some important elements of similarity and continuity in regard to reconciliation, yet with some radical differences. We have already noted that the term is used more frequently in the New Testament then the Old, and that the Revised Standard Version retains this usage from the King James in almost every instance instead of changing it to "atonement" as in the Old. We also discover that while reconciliation still means the overcoming of enmity and estrangement, in the New Testament it is centered mainly in the individual, and as the word Christian presupposes, it is centered in Christ as the agent.

Some problems of procedure confront us. Although as elsewhere reconciliation takes the form of the overcoming of alienation and hostility toward God, toward one's own inner self, toward one's fellows and toward one's total world, these seem more closely intertwined than before, and the possibility of separating them for discussion less logical. A second question has to do with biblical scholarship. Paul's letters are the earliest writing in the New Testament, antedating by at least a decade or more the first of the Gospels. Shall we then begin with Paul or with Jesus?

I have decided on something of a compromise—I hope a logical one. Since the specific references to reconciliation in the New Testament are almost all from the words of Paul, forming thereby the principal foundation of a Christian doctrine of atonement, this will be our first concern. It can probably be assumed that most of the readers of this book have a general familiarity with the life, ministry, teachings, death, and resurrection of Jesus as these are recorded in the Gospels. What cannot be so readily assumed is a definitive or agreed upon answer to the Christological question, and this has a considerable bearing on the doctrine of atonement. We shall therefore begin with some observations on what Jesus felt his relationship to God to be, and then examine Paul's views on reconciliation through Christ. In the second section we will deal with reconciliation in human relations as reflected in various parts of the New Testament.

Reconciliation as atonement through Christ

In what sense, if at all, did Jesus think of himself as the Son of God and the long-awaited Messiah? Though many books have been written on this question, it remains a disputed one. In John, the latest of the Gospels, he seems repeatedly to affirm his oneness with the Father, but in the Synoptics[1] he is far more reticent. He seems to imply it in Matthew 16:17. Yet only once in the Synoptic Gospels does he expressly affirm it. In Mark 14:62 in response to the high priest's question, "Are you the Christ, the Son of the Blessed?" he answers, "I am." In the corresponding passage in Matthew 26:64, the answer is "You have said so," and in Luke 22:70 "You say that I am." Such reticent responses, plus the many references of Jesus to himself as the Son of man in an apocalyptic setting, leave us with unanswered questions.

Since it is unlikely that any new evidence will appear, it is probable that opinions among scholars will remain divided. This being the case, we had better center attention on what can be known with certainty. It is certain from the records we have that Jesus believed himself called in a special way to proclaim both the love and the judgment of God, to witness to the kingdom of God, and to call those about him to enter it through faith and trust. It is certain that he lived in a close sense of intimacy with the Father from whom he drew his guidance and strength. It is certain that he died at the hands of evil and callous men, but in complete fidelity to what he believed to be the will of God. These certainties are enough to show the irrationality of the modern tendency to laud Jesus while discarding or radically modifying the God of Jesus.

These certainties are important ones, but they are not the only ones we have. It is certain that during his ministry Jesus lived a life of contagious love, that the power of God which he manifested transformed lives, both in body and spirit, and that after his death this same power continued in the fellowship of the church which bore his name. It is not surprising, therefore, that the early church was convinced that Jesus was "the anointed one," the Christ, and the Son of God. It would have been surprising, had they reached any other conclusion. And since this same power to transform lives has continued to the present, those who stand within the Christian tradition, and especially those to whom an experience of the living Christ is meaningful, do not hesitate to affirm it today.

If what has been said thus far is true, the Sonship of Jesus and the Saviorhood of Christ do not depend on impregnable biblical evidence as to what he said or did not say about his Messiahship, but on what he was and did and continues to do. *This* evidence does seem to me to be impregnable, and it was on this evidence that Paul rested his faith and erected his theological structure. So now let us turn to Paul.

Paul did not originate the belief that Jesus was the Christ, that God had raised him from the dead in a mighty victory over the sinfulness of men and the death of the body, and that in his death there was something of great moment to mankind. We find this note already being sounded in Peter's sermon at Pentecost on the birthday of the Church, which comes to its climax in the words, "Let all the house of Israel therefore know assuredly that God has made him both Lord and Christ, this Jesus whom you crucified." (Acts 2:36) It was not the rationalizing of a theological undertaking but a living experience which convinced Peter and the other disciples, who then became living witnesses for Christ at the cost of great suffering and eventual martyrdom. It was this experience also which won three thousand souls to Christ on the day of Pentecost, transforming a disparate and polyglot group into a joyous fellowship who shared their goods, worshipped and ate together "with glad and generous hearts, praising God and having favor with all the people."

Paul's experience can best be understood in the light of this background, his own radical experience of conversion, his Old Testament heritage, and his sense of the need to give a plausible explanation of what those of "the Way" were experiencing. Leave out any of these factors, and much of what he says about the reconciling death of Christ is apt to appear cryptic and unsatisfying. Yet what he was aiming at was a matter of deep truth and of permanent worth.

The struggle with sin and the inability of the law to overcome it, so vividly portrayed at the end of Romans 7, is probably autobiographical. In any case, Paul was speaking from experience when he wrote in II Corinthians 5:17, "If anyone is in Christ, he is a new creation; the old has passed away, behold, the new has come." New, yet not wholly new. Paul was a Jew, "a Pharisee, a son of Pharisees" (Acts 23:6) and both the early purification rites through the blood of slain offerings and the later forms of temple ritual were part of his heritage. To say that he made the death of Jesus simply another blood sacrifice for sin is to malign Paul; it is unrealistic to suppose that there was no connection in his thinking. He gave fresh meaning to ancient ways of thinking, and did this in a context more congenial to the thought patterns of his time than to ours.

As Paul wrestled with the problem of how to give expression for new Christians to the saving power of God in Christ, it seems to me that he made two mistakes which have been transmitted to beset Christian theology through the centuries. One of these is an overemphasis on the death of Christ to the exclusion of attention to the life and ministry of Jesus. To be sure, Paul could not quote the Synoptic Gospels, for they had not been written yet, but he must have been familiar with much of the life story of Jesus through his association with Peter and others and the oral tradition circulated in the churches. More of this should have appeared in his writing to keep the balance true. The death of Jesus followed by the resurrection was indeed crucial, as is evident from the attention given to these events in all the Gospels. Yet the death of this man would have been simply that of one more Jew who offended the authorities and was executed for disturbing the *status quo,* were it not for what Jesus was and did and taught during his ministry. About this Paul is strangely silent.

His second error lies in his virtual introduction of the doctrine of original sin as an inherited curse from Adam's disobedience. After the story of Adam's fall in Genesis 3, the Old Testament has practically nothing to say about the origin of sin. There is a glancing reference to Adam in Hosea 6:7 and in KJV but not RSV in Job 31:33, but nothing like a doctrine of an inherited curse. What Paul did was to derive a doctrine from Genesis 3, and thus it became fastened upon centuries of subsequent Christian thought. Christian faith and belief would have been better off without it.

Yet if these were mistakes, other elements in Paul's thought contained much truth and permanent relevance. The basic notes in his view of reconciliation through Christ were the overcoming of man's enmity against God, the forgiveness of sin with a reordering of the moral life, and deliverance from evil powers by victory over them. While these notes are found mingled in Paul's letters, we can, for convenience, look at them separately.

The overcoming of enmity has to do with man's enmity toward God, not the reverse. Where the concept of divine wrath appears in Paul's words, which are few compared with the concept's frequency in the Old Testament, it connotes the hatred of divine love toward the sin, not the sinner, and it is God's love which has prompted the sending of his Son to die for the ungodly. This distinction is crucial, for a doctrine of atonement to propitiate the wrath of an angry God has long held sway in Christian thought. Paul believed that Christ's death opened the way to an expiation of human sin. But in expiation the change takes place in man, not in God.

The order is clear if we will look carefully at the key passage in II Corinthians 5:17-19. "God . . . through Christ reconciled us to himself and gave us the ministry of reconciliation; . . . God was in Christ reconciling the world to himself, not counting their trespasses against them, and entrusting to us the message of reconciliation." It is *we* and the *world,* not God, who are in need of reconciliation.

Paul does not attempt to say how the sacrificial death of Christ is efficacious. Perhaps he did not think it either necessary or possible to say, but he knew the result in his own life. From his references to the blood of Christ, it would not be surprising if he made some connection betweeen this and the earlier rite of cleansing from sin through a blood sacrifice. If so, he transformed without eliminating this part of his heritage.

Paul is much clearer as to what is required of one who desires to be reconciled. He must accept this miracle of grace by faith, trustfully and penitently. It is a free gift, not to be earned by obedience to the Law. We are "bought with a price," and God accepts the unworthy. "Therefore, since we are justified by faith, we have peace with God through our Lord Jesus Christ." (Rom. 5:1) But it is not a passive peace; God requires continuing effort toward a life of moral strength and purity.

It is in the forgiveness of sin when one turns to God in penitence and faith that the overcoming of man's alienation from God is centered. But what is sin? In part, Paul views sin as an objective thing in the nature of man. It appears to be this in much of his discussion of forgiveness and acceptance by God, as if to say "Sin comes in through Adam, out through Christ." Romans 5:6-21 reads this way. Yet in Rom. 5:1-5 it has a more personal character as the fruits of its conquest are recounted. In Romans 7 there is a personal wrestling with sin and resulting guilt, with a futile struggle to master it through the law, which the more objective references to man's sinful state do not carry. Furthermore, Paul's frequent moral injunctions to the churches, including such catalogs of sins as are found in Rom. 1:29-30, Gal. 5:19-21 and Col. 3:5-8, give ample evidence that as a man and a pastoral counselor, if not as a theologian, he had a vivid sense of the personal nature of sins as well as of the objective fact of sin. Yet in these, as in life's vicissitudes, we can be "more than conquerors through him who loved us."

Not only in Paul's thought does Christ effect the reconciliation of man to God by bridging the rift of man's alienation and making possible the forgiveness of sin with a new life resulting, but he vanquishes the evil powers. This brings us to the third main note in Paul's thought—the exultant note of Christ's glorious triumph over all that assails the spirit of man.

In part, these are the "principalities and powers" of which Paul speaks so frequently. (Rom. 8:38; Col. 1:16; 2:15; and Eph. 3:10; 6:12 if Ephesians may be credited to Paul.[2]) Paul does not define them, but he apparently felt them to be cosmic forces "in the heavenly places," and demons surrounding and engulfing men. They are his theoretical answer to the unexplained evil in the world, though from the standpoint of Christian experience, Christ has conquered them. But there are also much more immediate and less mysterious forces over which Christ is victor: sin and death.

Paul regarded death as having entered the world as the penalty of man's sin. Hence, the conquest of sin brought the conquest of death. Paul speaks of immortality, but not in the Greek sense of its being the inalienable endowment of all men. If we so regard it, as we may from the inference that a God of infinite love would not condemn any of his human creatures to nothingness, this is on another basis than Paul's. Yet he does speak of it, along with more frequent references to resurrection elsewhere, in the most glorious hymn of victory over death that was ever penned in I Corinthians 15.

In Col. 1:15-20 Paul has a message of great depth, though

we could wish him to have spelled it out more fully. This is the reconciliation of "all things" through Christ, "whether on earth or in heaven, making peace by the blood of his cross." In this he seems to intimate the conquest not only of the principalities and powers and the immediate assailants of the human spirit but of the entire world, in the creation of which Christ has been God's agent. This suggests an alienation of the totality of things from God's design and the need of a cosmic peace.

In summation, Paul did much to set the tenor of belief in the cross as the central symbol of Christian faith and life. It should be central—no sensitive Christian would want to dethrone it or the work of Christ for man's salvation which it symbolizes. Yet we need not accept to the letter every aspect of Paul's interpretation of it. We do well to accept and to live by the consummate notes of Christ's self-giving in life and in death, and his continuing victory over enmity and alienation, over sin and pain and death and every evil power that can assail us. If we will do this, some differences of opinion as to a doctrine of atonement need not divide us.

Reconciliation in human relations

We come now to the more clear-cut, and some would say more practical, subject of reconciliation in human relations as indices of it are found in the New Testament. Here, indisputably, we must begin with Jesus.

Jesus felt it to be his vocation to lead men away from sin, strife, and shallow living by making available to them the forgiving and accepting grace of God. This he embodied in his central message of the kingdom of God and the conditions of its entrance, about which we gather from the Synoptic Gospels that he spoke far more than he did about himself. What Jesus did throughout his ministry was to proclaim and to manifest a gospel of reconciliation to God, to other persons, and to one's own sinful, distraught or lethargic self.

This message Jesus proclaimed in his total ministry both by words and the events of his living. It is imbedded in that collection of sayings which we call the Sermon on the Mount and in many parables. Some of his parables deal with reconciliation more explicitly than others as, for example, the parable of the unforgiving servant in Matt. 18: 23-35, which makes it evident that in Jesus' thinking there was no place for "cheap grace." The tender story in Luke 7:36-50 of the forgiveness of the woman who brought her tribute of love puts the same thought in a positive setting. So does the possibly spurious story in John 8:1-11 of the woman taken in adultery, which whether authentic or not reflects the spirit of understanding grace which characterized his ministry. The same may be said of his own climactic word from the cross in Luke 23:34, "Father, forgive them, for they know not what they do."

It appears certain that Jesus linked the forgiveness of sin by God with the willingness to forgive others. Not only is this evident in his reply to Peter's question in Matt. 18: 21-22, but we affirm it every time we say the Lord's prayer. Indeed, such forgiveness on the human level is both the precondition and the fruit of divine forgiveness.

Changed lives were the result of personal fellowship with Jesus and response to both his teaching and his love expressed in friendship, understanding, and good will. Touched by his confidence and outgoing love, sinners became good men, the proud became humble, the weak became strong, the fearful and anxious found new faith and hope. But not all did—there is the tragedy of Judas and the fickleness of the crowd between Palm Sunday and Good Friday. Yet enough responded and remained new persons, upheld both by their recollections of Jesus and their resurrection faith in his living presence, to give us both the Christian church and the New Testament.

As indicated in the previous section, it is essential to stress the reconciling nature of the living and the teaching of Jesus, for apart from what preceded it his death would have been no more than the unfortunate early death of a misunderstood, if not misguided, young Jew who tangled with the authorities and got himself into trouble as a dangerous revolutionary figure. We need to see the life, the message, the death and the resurrection of Jesus all as part of one supreme event in human history—an event in which we find the supreme disclosure of the nature and long purposes of God.

But as we need to see his life and ministry as an essential element in the total Christ event, so we need to view his words in conjunction with this total ministry and disclosure of God. The most explicit words which were recorded as spoken by Jesus on reconciliation are in Matthew 5:23-24: "So if you are offering your gift at the altar, and there remember that your brother has something against you, leave your gift there before the altar and go; first be reconciled to your brother, and then come and offer your gift." This is often interpreted as putting right human relations above worship. This does not accord with the attitude of Jesus as we find it everywhere in his ministry. Rather, it is a protest against a barren worship in which human relations are left out. To Jesus, God came first and right human relations in obedient love flow from our love of God and devotion to his will.

It is important also to note the words "and there remember that *your brother has something against you.*" As the words were originally spoken and became lodged in the memory of the hearers, the context was most directly the tensions with a fellow Jew as "brother." But there is no indication that Jesus would thus restrict it. Certainly it need not be thus limited. This word is of universal application today to the rifts between nations, between black and white, rich and poor, younger and older, employer and employed, husband and wife, friend and friend, and between those involved in any other sort of human rift. There is bound to be fault on one side or the other, usually on both, and it is well to consider that the brother "may have something against you." And to the mind of Jesus, the kind of worship which moves one to self-examination and the spirit of reconciliation is an essential part of human living.

The parable which gives the fullest amplification of Matt. 5:23-24 is the parable of the Good Samaritan in Luke 10:29-37. It is too familiar to require much amplification. Directly following as it does the enunciation of the two great commandments, it defines "neighbor," and by implication "brother," in terms which cut across all earthly barriers.

In Matthew 18:21 Peter asks "Lord, how often shall my brother sin against me, and I forgive him? As many as seven times?" The striking hyperbole with which Jesus replies clearly means, in more prosaic terms, "without limit." Yet we are not to suppose that Jesus meant that we should let evil go unchecked. The much disputed words in the Sermon on the Mount, "Do not resist one who is evil" (Matt. 5:39) with the injunctions which follow as to the smitten cheek, the extracted garment, and the second mile are admittedly difficult sayings to interpret. Yet it is important to note that Jesus does not enjoin nonresistance to evil. From what precedes and follows these words, we are justified in assuming that the burden of these passages is resistance through love and the conquest of evil through nonviolent expressions of love.

There are numerous references to peace in the Gospels,

ranging from the song of the angels on the first Christmas morning to the tender, moving words of the Last Supper discourse. Times without number, the apparently disparate sayings of Jesus in Matt. 10:34 and Matt. 26:52 have been quoted against each other on the legitimacy of military conflict. Taken in their proper settings both are true, for Jesus saw with great realism that fidelity to him and his cause would engender conflict while with equal realism he saw the ineffectiveness of the sword to bring about reconciliation or the conditions where peace could prevail.

Without attempting to comment on all the references to peace recorded as spoken by Jesus, two call for special mention. One of these is in Mark 9:50, with a turn which makes it worthy of more attention than I have often heard given to it, "Have salt in yourselves, and be at peace with one another." The other is the dramatic incident on the morning of the first Palm Sunday. We are told that as Jesus "drew near and saw the city he wept over it, saying 'Would that even today you knew the things that make for peace! But now they are hid from your eyes.'" (Luke 19:41-42) A truer prophet than his contemporaries, he foresaw the destruction of the Holy City which, in less than forty years, was to be laid waste by the Roman legions. One may still see in the Roman Forum the Arch of Titus which was erected to commemorate the victory of military power over Jewish nationalism.

Of all the sayings of Jesus which speak poignantly for the spirit of reconciliation in the midst of human conflict, the most exacting and at the same time the most needful is that of Matthew 5:43-48, which contains the injunction "Love your enemies and pray for those who persecute you, so that you may be sons of your Father who is in heaven." Even in a biblically illiterate generation, most people are aware that Jesus said some such words. But acted upon? Not often to any great extent, either by the professed followers of Christ or others. The injunction runs too deeply counter to social custom and to our egocentricity and self-defensiveness. It is easier to dismiss the words as a lovely but unattainable ideal. As we become more spiritually mature, we may discover their profound realism, for the opposite is the way of death—the death of happiness, of spiritual excellence, of social stability, and, in time of war, of great numbers of human lives.

We must now look more briefly at other significant pointers toward reconciliation to be found in other parts of the New Testament. A good place to begin is the book of Acts, for it gives a vibrant witness to the spirit of reconciliation as this had come upon the young church when, Spirit-filled, it went out from the gathering at Pentecost to begin a new way of life. From the beginning, those of "the Way" shared their prayers, their praises, and their property. Soon they worked out an amicable division of labor to take care of their duties and see that none were left in need. As Stephen, one of these first deacons of the church, came to his death by martyrdom, he was able to say in the spirit of his risen Master, "Lord, do not hold this sin against them." (Acts 7:60)

From the beginning the disciples were arrested almost daily, sometimes admonished and let go, sometimes jailed for considerable periods. They used these occasions to give their witness to Christ, and while the defenses recorded show much vigor, they are remarkably free from bitterness. Paul, to be sure, could call Elymas the magician "you son of the devil" (Acts 13:10) and the high priest Ananias "you whitewashed wall" (Acts 23:3), but somehow this does not detract from the dignity with which he labored incessantly for Christ, preached with great discernment to the Athenians on Mars Hill, made his defense before Felix

49

and Agrippa, and was master of the situation at the shipwreck.

There was not always full agreement among the leaders, but any differences are minor compared with the way in which they maintained "the unity of the spirit in the bond of peace." (Eph. 4:3) The conference at Jerusalem recorded in Acts 15 is one of the most important gatherings ever held, for it made possible the merging of Jew and Gentile in the nascent church. This was foreshadowed in symbolic fashion by the meeting of Peter and Cornelius, and Peter's word, "Truly I perceive that God shows no partiality" (Acts 10:34) is a truth much in need of being acted upon in today's divided world.

But what of Paul's words on the reconciliation of person to person as we find them in his letters? Actually, we find him using the word in this connection only once, and that in a passage in which he attempted some marriage counseling. In I Cor. 7:10-11 we find: "To the married I give charge, not I but the Lord, that the wife should not separate from her husband (but if she does, let her remain single or else be reconciled to her husband)—and that the husband should not divorce his wife." Circumstances differ so much that probably this need not be taken as a word from the Lord for all time! Yet the matter was important then, and it still is in many households.

Paul repeatedly counsels the churches against contention and disharmony. Yet these specific passages are dwarfed by Paul's supreme contribution to the spirit of reconciliation in human relations, I Corinthians 13. Unquestionably one of the greatest passages in the Bible, it is also one of the greatest in all literature. Taken seriously and lived up to in what it both enjoins and affirms, it could transform our broken world.

Two other passages of great importance, which may or

may not have been written by Paul, are found in the letter to the Ephesians. In Eph. 2:12-17 the author speaks of a new unity in Christ and says, "For he is our peace, who has made us both one, and has broken down the dividing wall of hostility." The hostility is apparently between Jew and Gentile, but the other rifts in human relations can equally well be covered by it. The King James version puts in a striking phrase the way in which both parties have been reconciled to God: "in one body by the cross, having slain the enmity thereby." In Eph. 4:1-16 there is a magnificent call to unity in the one body and one Spirit of Christ. No wonder it is read so often in ecumenical gatherings today!

One might appropriately stop with a reference to these climactic statements of enduring truth and value. But I wish to cite one more of a very practical nature, for it is "the little foxes that spoil the vineyards." (Song. 2:15) In the book of James, we are told that the tongue is a fire. "How great a forest is set ablaze by a small fire!" (3:5) There are greater words than these in the Bible, but there are none truer. Many of the quarrels, disputes, and dissensions of the world are started and all are intensified by angry and bitter words. Words can cut deep wounds, whether in personal, political, or other kinds of human relations. Yet the right words, provided they are genuine and wise and flow from a Christ-spirit of reconciliation, can go far toward healing the wounds of the world. If we have such words to speak, let us not withhold them.

4. RECONCILIATION
IN THE INDIVIDUAL PERSON

It has been stated repeatedly in the earlier chapters that reconciliation in the full sense requires reconciliation with God, with other persons, with one's self, and with one's world. However, the biblical insights on these themes have been traced under two categories rather than four. There is a reason for this. What the Bible says on reconciliation is not neatly categorized. What it says, even on man's relation to God and neighbor, has to be separated for the sake of orderly discussion; it is merged in the Bible. There is still less of a separation in the biblical point of view between what happens in the inner life and one's total outlook through faith, obedience, and an attempt to live in love and loyalty to the Highest.

However, the modern mind requires that we look more specifically at what the human psyche is and does. Psychology and psychotherapy have made great advances in our time. There are variations within the schools of thought in these fields. In the earlier stages with a strong emphasis on naturalism, behaviorism, and determinism which left little place, if any, for the human spirit and none for God, there was not much of a meeting-point between the exponents of this approach and of the Christian faith and gospel.

This is now changed considerably, and the findings of psychotherapists are an important, and even necessary, part of the equipment of the pastoral counselor. Some psychotherapists believe in the personal God of the Bible and Christian faith, though others do not, but there is a vital common ground in the human spirit.

After a preliminary survey of the plight we are in, the procedure in this chapter will be to present the basic notes in the Christian understanding of man with the corresponding psychological picture. Then we shall try to see what religion and psychology together can do if the souls of men are to come to their fullest health and find inner peace with themselves and their world.

Man against himself

Some years ago one of the most noted psychoanalysts of our time, Erich Fromm, wrote a widely influential book entitled *Man for Himself*. It contains much valuable material to which we shall later make some references, for while its author espouses a humanistic rather than a theistic ethic and understanding of man, he makes a large place for objective moral values and for productive and healthy living. I mention it at this point to suggest that as one surveys the contemporary scene, man *against* himself might be the more apt description.

Sigmund Freud, along with contributions which have made him the father of modern psychoanalysis, made much of the repression of the sexual impulse as a cause of human disorders. The ablest psychologists of today think he overstated this point, but its popularization has left a residuum in modern culture. Whatever the reasons, there is now a minimal amount of sexual repression, whether in the young or many of their elders. Are we the healthier for this shift in modes of sexual thought and action? This must be doubted in view of the degree to which biological impulse in the area of sex has replaced its sacredness and fruition in happy and lasting marriages. In this quest for erotic indulgence, there is a case of "man against himself."

The late Karen Horney in *The Neurotic Personality of Our Time* and numerous other psychoanalysts have located the roots of neurotic personality in anxiety. This can be either a conscious anxiety about objective or anticipated conditions, or a dull but destructive inner unhappiness, or, as often happens, an unconscious anxiety which projects itself outward in hostility toward those nearest. There is obviously plenty of all kinds of anxiety around in the contemporary world. The impending threat of atomic destruction, so much in the foreground in the years immediately following the emergence of the nuclear age, is less talked about today than the dangers of overpopulation and the pollution and destruction of the environment. Nevertheless, all three hang over our heads like the sword of Damocles.[1] For many there is a more immediate source of anxiety in the war in Vietnam, with the drafting of hundreds of thousands of youth at a critical time in their lives and the death to the time of writing of more than 40,000 of the American boys. There is a serious dislocation of the economy by high prices, high taxes and a high interest rate with a fall-off in the value of stocks, which has diminished the economic security of many whose savings of a lifetime are thus imperiled. There are millions of hungry people, not only in underdeveloped nations but in America.

In addition to such objective conditions, there is the anxiety induced in a highly competitive society by both economic and cultural factors. One feels he must make himself a successful and hence a financially valuable person in business, industry, or the professions, even at the cost of moral principles and of bodily and mental health. Fromm calls this suggestively "the marketing orientation" in the character of modern man. There are major, and often violent, clashes among various segments of society among both those who are promoting changes in society and those who wish to keep it as it is. There is also a large-scale, and apparently mounting, distrust of the government, and especially of its bureaucracies, which no amount of rhetoric from those in power will dispel. There is an alarming rise in the crime rate, at the same time a cause, an effect, and a symptom of current anxiety and unrest. Add to such factors as these man's persistent anxieties as to his social status, his family relations, his health, his coming old age and death, and there is plenty of occasion for man to be "against himself," and as a consequence against others.

To refer to another influential book, *Man's Search for Meaning* by Viktor Frankl, there is another and a very important reason for man to be against himself—a loss or at least a lack of a belief that life as a whole has any meaning. In part this is due to the confused and painful conditions amongst which men live, and these are dramatically illustrated in the first half of the book by Dr. Frankl's observations as he witnessed the reactions of his fellow prisoners in a Nazi concentration camp. But it is also due to a belief, either naïve or philosophically arrived at, that life is empty of meaning with no undergirding foundations. With this comes a loss of the meaning of love, of suffering, and of life's potentialities.

There can be little doubt that this has widely occurred in our time, among the affluent, the comfortable, the socially accepted and those relatively free from bodily or other ills, as well as those more limited by particular circumstances. Then when one or another of life's vicissitudes befalls them, these troubled persons have no ground to stand on. The theater and the novels of our day, as well as the more explicit statements of philosophical and psychological existentialists, have made this evident.

Aside from all such weighty matters, there are many things that make people nervous and thus can turn one simultaneously against himself and others. There are the ever-present noises that impinge on us in most urban situations. There is overcrowding, jostling, and a lack of privacy, whether in inadequate housing, the subway rush, or the rat race on the freeways that many must combat both morning and night. There is the hurry of getting off to work, often after too little sleep, and the hurry of things that must be done all day, often routine things that induce boredom rather than a sense of creativity. At home fatigue produces irritability, often with misunderstandings and hurt feelings. The radio and the television are sometimes relaxing, but with bad news of the world and trashy commercials are often quite the contrary. Where there are children, there are both the anxieties and the forms of disturbance incident to their growing up. And much more.

This is by no means to say that everything is wrong with modern life, or that everybody becomes a neurotic or unreconciled personality under the impingement of these factors. The marvel is that so many remain in reasonably good psychic health, barring the headaches and tensions of which the TV commercials are ever reminding us, as they promote pain-killers and tranquilizers for their alleviation. Nor is the social situation all bad—of its good side we shall say more in later chapters. Yet it is clear that all is not well with modern man. "Man against himself" describes much that prevails in the attitudes of millions of our contemporaries, and perhaps in ourselves.

Where this state of mind exists the result is irritability, if not outright hostility, distrust of one's self which one tries to cover up, and distrust of others which becomes overt. Its harvest is a kind of dull despair which cripples the abundant life of which Jesus spoke—the productive life, if one prefers a more psychological term.[2] At this point, reconciliation with one's self and with one's world is an imperative need. But how is this to be brought about?

The answers are to be found both in Christian faith and in the best of psychological knowledge—not in an either/or but in a both/and. In both approaches, the answers are rooted in a clear understanding of the nature of man. To this matter we now turn. In outlining a Christian understanding of human nature, we shall note agreements with, and differences from, a secular psychological approach insofar as these are relevant to man's inner reconciliation.

The Christian understanding of man

This topic is of great importance to the possibilities and procedures of reconciliation in any sense. Obviously, in a few pages we can only touch the fringes of it, but the main outlines may be stated.

a. *Made in the divine image.* There are great truths to be discerned in the poetic, mythological language of the first chapter of Genesis. One of its most permanently meaningful statements is in Genesis 1:27, "So God created man in his own image, in the image of God he created him; male and female he created them." While the first part of this statement is symbolic in contrast with the more obvious realism of the second, it is not less true. But what is the divine image?

There are anthropomorphic elements in the Bible which attribute acts and attitudes to God that are all too human. Yet taken as a whole, the nature of God is disclosed in the highest insights of both the Old and New Testaments as a deity who is altogether loving and at the same time just and righteous, infinite in goodness, wisdom, and creative power, always concerned for his erring people, and compassionate in their troubles. Man is pictured as departing again and again from what God intends him to be and to do; yet he is God's supreme creation, of supreme worth as the object of God's love, given dominion over the rest of God's creation and crowned with glory and honor. Numerous passages reflect this picture, but none more vividly than the eighth Psalm, which takes on special relevance today as man's mastery of space discloses new marvels of both physical nature and of man's ability:

> When I look at thy heavens, the work of thy fingers,
>   the moon and the stars which thou hast established;
> what is man that thou art mindful of him,
>   and the son of man that thou dost care for him?
> Yet thou hast made him little less than God,
>   and dost crown him with glory and honor.
> Thou hast given him dominion over the works of thy hands;
>   thou hast put all things under his feet. . . . (8:3-6)

In modern diction, the biblical view of man is of a creature with vast potentialities, with creative work to do and with the need to give a high priority to love, to moral values, and to the quest for truth about himself and the world he lives in. This is what the best of modern psychiatry says about man, though usually without attempting to say anything about God.

b. *Nature and spirit.* Basic to anything else that can be said about man is the blend of nature and spirit within him. This is often called mind and body, or body and soul, but nature and spirit are more inclusive terms.

Each individual human being is one unitary being with two inseparably related aspects. This is what the Bible presupposes without the dualism which was to creep in later from Platonic thought. It is the position of the major psychologists today, though often without the biblical and Judeo-Christian conviction of the relation of the human to the divine Creator-spirit.

There is less agreement as to how man's nature and spirit are related to each other. Systems have been devised which bear such names as behaviorism, epiphenomenalism, self-psychology, psychophysical parallelism, interaction, and gestalt. It would not be profitable here to discuss the fine points of these systems.[3] It is not necessary to do so, for in recent years the emphasis has shifted away from the attempt to give a single explanation of the phenomenon of man to a more realistic appraisal of man in his entirety. Man is both nature and spirit, and in spite of other differences this view is in general shared by the exponents of psychology, socialogy, ethics, and religion and by ordinary people who know themselves to be able to say "I" and mean by this pronoun that in them there is a body but more than a body.

That man is a part of nature in the sense of being a biological organism, the highest of the animals in the evolutionary scale of development, hardly needs defense. Man's physiological structure with its intricate combination of bones, blood, muscles, cellular tissues, sense organs and internal organs is very much like that of the higher mammals, though often with less acute sensory equipment and always with a more complex brain and nervous system. Furthermore, man shares with the other animals three very basic drives: hunger, self-preservation, and the sexual impulse. Yet even when these similarities have been recognized, there are still great differences. Helpless at birth, man has the longest infancy of any, and during the years of growth to maturity he acquires what no animal could: a personality. Lacking the range of instincts by which the animal, often amazingly, adapts himself to his environment and fulfills his bodily functions, the human being is equipped with potentialities vastly more amazing. These are what constitute the human spirit.

Spirit is that in man which makes him distinctively human. It is not to be identified with "the spiritual life" in a religious sense, though it includes it. Man's capacity for worship and for obedience to the leadings of an invisible, transcendent but present Spirit, is one of the most distinctive aspects of the human spirit. Man's spiritual nature is found in his capacity for self-awareness, self-understanding, and self-criticism, and hence in his capacity to transcend the lower impulses of his nature in pursuit of higher ideals and goals. It is present in man's capacity to judge between conflicting values in any field, and thus to make decisions as to the better or the worse.

Spirit is also man's capacity for abstract thought and the use of reason both in and beyond his immediate needs. It is found not only in man's ability to discern meanings, but to communicate with others through language symbols. In memories of his own past and in the power to learn from his cultural heritage, in anticipation of and in planning for the future, man transcends time even though he must live in the demands of the present. In creative imagination and by the use of intelligence and effort, he is able in a measure to reshape his environment. Although man's ability to master physical nature is not unlimited, it is so great that it is futile to set limits.

The human spirit may also be described by the ancient trilogy of the good, the true, and the beautiful. Man can both create beauty and be lifted by it. He is unique in his concern for truth and in his power not only to appropriate but to create great systems of truth in the sciences, the humanities and other fields of human interest. Yet most important of all, from the standpoint of his ability to live harmoniously with himself and his fellowmen, he has a conscience and a sense of moral values which can be distorted but never fully lost as long as one is a sane human being. In its right direction and in living that is consistent with the right lies his and his society's salvation.

Everything in the preceding paragraphs constitutes what is meant by the human spirit. It is not shared with the lower animals, or with any machine, however marvelous the exploits of the computer, or with anything else in inanimate nature. Too glowing a list of attributes, in view of the sordidness we sometimes see? These are human potentialities, and though their development may be curtailed through a network of circumstances, these potentialities are found in the humblest person, and every person, whatever his achievements or maturity, has worth and dignity as a person.

c. *Freedom and responsibility.* We noted above as an essential characteristic of the human spirit man's capacity for making decisions among competing claims. His behavior is not primarily instinctual as an animal's is to a far greater degree, nor is it mechanical like the machines which man himself has produced in great abundance. Man's power to choose between alternative ideas, values, and courses of action constitutes his freedom. From his freedom stems his moral responsibility, for without it he could not be held accountable for anything he does.

It is only because man has some freedom of choice that he can decide between good and evil and direct his actions accordingly, employ his intelligence to discover truth, become sensitive to beauty and love, appropriate meanings from the past or project them as goals into the future, and increase the values of the society around him. Furthermore, it is only through freedom that he can come into a conscious relationship with God.

The freedom of the human spirit is the supreme endowment of man and the supreme gift of God. Yet no person is wholly free. The infant is a little bundle of living protoplasm unable to do anything except eat and sleep and express his bodily needs with a cry. Yet because of his potential, he is still human. As he grows older he acquires freedom as he acquires personality, and with this freedom a measure of moral responsibility. As he comes to adult life, he is still not wholly free, not only because of bodily or mental limitations and the restraints imposed by the conditions around him, but because of what has happened to him and in him in the intervening years.

At this point a basic difference emerges among those who seek to pass judgment on the nature of man. On the one hand, the view of determinism is that *all* man's decisions and actions, if consistently held, even his thoughts, are the result of one's bodily inheritance as this has been molded by one's past and present environment. This is likely to be the position of those who believe that a scientific approach to the problems of man and society requires it. On the other side are those who are ready enough to admit the influence of such factors, and therefore the need to provide a better environment for all. But they still believe that without a measure of freedom of will, there can be no true creativity, no rational judgment, and no moral responsibility.

An attempted compromise is sometimes made by psychologists and sociologists, as for example by Erich Fromm[4] who says that a person's character is determined by his innate vitality and the degree of acceptance or resistance which this gives him to the environmental forces which play upon him from early childhood. Our decisions are then determined by our character. Yet since man, and man alone, is endowed with reason and conscience, we are not helpless victims of circumstance but can change both the inner and outer aspects of our living. This seems to me like an attempt to bring in freedom on deterministic foundations, and it might be both simpler and more consistent to say that in man's reason and conscience his freedom is primarily located. In any case, we go on thinking and acting *as if* we were free to do otherwise, and except in early childhood or in abnormal conditions of physical or mental health, society holds us responsible for our behavior.

d. *The individual in society.* Every individual lives in some kind of social structure, and whether he approves it or not, he is a part of it. He can flee from one social group to another, and in rare instances to solitary living, but he can never escape wholly from social connections. It would not be necessary to press this point except to point out certain important results.

First, every person *is* an individual, a unique person not exactly like any other. His personhood is as unique as his fingerprints. Identical twins, born of the same parents and the same living cell and reared in almost if not completely the same environment, are nevertheless two persons, each with an identity and a character of his own. This means that every person should be treated as a person and not simply a constituent in an anonymous, faceless corporate mass. Not only is this true in human relations, but it reinforces the Christian view that God loves every individual person, not simply humanity as a whole.

Second, society often provides an easy alibi for an individual's discomfiture. If one feels at odds with himself—anxious, troubled and unable to make a go of life—he looks for a scapegoat. After many years now of popularizing the deterministic view, it is not difficult for him to blame his parents, the raw deals he has had in life, his school or church experiences, his spouse, the job he is in, or the total impact of an unjust society. In greater or less degree these charges may be true. Yet the result is an inevitable hostility which bars the door to reconciliation both with himself and with those he blames for his plight. He must either change the circumstances or learn to live with them. To change them may not be easy, and a large part of society's problems today hinge on whether the methods used are the right ones. We must give much attention to this issue in the chapters which follow. The second alternative—to learn to accept one's self within the circumstances—is not an easy matter, either. A true acceptance does not mean a passive complacency, which is too often espoused under the aegis of "adjustment," but an inner readjustment. Writing from a Roman dungeon from which he was soon to go to his death, Paul calls it "the peace of God, which passes all understanding." (Phil. 4: 7)

e. *Man as sinner.* We come now to a category for which psychologists rarely have a place. Guilt, yes, for it is common enough to have a guilty conscience, and an extreme state of guilt can wreck one's personality. But not sin.

There are a number of reasons for this avoidance of the terminology of sin by those who deal professionally with disturbances of the human spirit. The basic reason is that sin connotes not simply wrongdoing, but disobedience to God, and whatever the personal attitudes of the scientist, God has no place in either the natural or social sciences. Furthermore, disobedience suggests an authoritarian conscience, an effort to please an external authority, which the psychologist says should be replaced by self-direction. Many are committed to the relativity of all human values, which leaves no ground for being judgmental. And in addition to these theoretical factors, many would say that to tell a person he is a sinner wounds rather than heals a sick personality.

Psychologists differ among themselves as to whether there is an innate impulse in man to evil as well as good. Freud, after the first World War, was so impressed with the power of the destructive impulse that he came to regard this as one of man's instinctual urges, with a "death instinct" capable of being turned either outward or inward. Most psychoanalysts today do not follow him in this, and reject completely the traditional Christian belief in original sin.

In the preceding chapter, we saw that the doctrine of original sin owes its origin primarily to Paul, and we are not obligated to follow him in it. But must the Christian understanding of man give up the whole idea of sin? If it does, it gives up a large part of the Bible, for its basic note is man's sinfulness and God's steadfast love in spite of it—a love which makes possible forgiveness and coming to new life through acceptance of God's grace.

As for the authoritarian conscience, the nature of the authority makes a great difference. The God whom Jesus worshiped, served, and revealed is not an arbitrary despot but a loving Father ever opening to his children new possibilities of love, truth, and creative living. "The Lawgiver is not the source of arbitrary, imposed moral rules, established once and for all from on high, but the establisher of ever-new possibilities of righteousness which both destroy and fulfill generalizations based upon the past." [5]

We can learn much from the psychotherapists. We do not need to talk about God in every counseling session; everybody ought to develop a mature conscience which will be self-directed toward the right; understanding love is better in its motives and more effective in its results than blame. But does this mean that we must give up the idea of man as sinner against both God and neighbor? I think not.

The distinctive character of the ethical outlook of Jesus as he lived in intimate fellowship with God and obedience to his will was that faith and morals are all of one piece. On the affirmative side, love of neighbor is the fruit of love of God; on the negative, to hate or to wrong other persons is to sin against God. Although what is thought to be sin may vary from time to time and from person to person, we had better not dispense with the idea of sin. There are sinful acts and attitudes; there are sins of overt action and sins of indifference and complacency; there are social sins in which great masses of people sin against other groups of people. The need of reconciliation, whether inward or outward, is much related to sin, though this is not its only source. And if, in addition to neurosis and other psychic ills, sin is a realistic part of the human predicament we must take it seriously.

f. *The possibility of redemption.* Basic to the Christian understanding of man is the belief that life can be radically changed. Both the burden of self-centeredness so vividly portrayed by its opposite in I Corinthians 13 and the inner turmoil in which one so often finds himself can be lifted. One then finds a new inner motivation, new sources of strength, a new outlook on the world, a new joy through the grace of God. Christ is the bearer of this grace, both as pattern and power for living. Where Christian experience is real and life-transforming, God "accepts the unacceptable," to use Tillich's memorable phrase. This is at the heart of the Christian doctrine of justification by faith.

Yet seldom, if ever, does this occur without human agents. The person being changed must cooperate with an act of will, and he needs a human agent to set forth the new possibilities and by loving concern help to engender the faith that leads to redemption. Much of the remainder of the chapter will deal with the processes of reconciliation in the inner life through the conjunction of divine grace, personal response, and a mediating agency.

Reconciliation in psychotherapy and religion

In the earlier sections of this chapter numerous references have been made to psychiatry and psychotherapy. The author claims no professional competence in this field, but there are aspects of it that are available to the layman. It will be useful to look at these in relation to the theology and practice of the Christian faith.

While there are major agreements in the understanding of man as being more than a biological organism, as an individual in society and capable of change, the secular psychotherapists usually hold to a theoretical determinism, even though they regard man as a responsible being with some freedom of self-direction. Without a concept of sin or of either creation or redemption through a divine agency, can the two fields get together?

There is evidence that they do get together in pastoral counseling. This has become a part of the curriculum in virtually every theological seminary, and with varying success ministers do a large amount of counseling in their parish relations. But can they do so without a lurking inconsistency? This problem is tackled head on by Thomas C. Oden in *Kerygma and Counseling,* with not only an affirmative answer but a somewhat surprising correlation between Karl Barth's doctrine of revelation and Carl Rogers' client-centered therapy. However, I wish only to state a few convictions of my own.

I do not see any possibility of a consistent adaptation of the Christian understanding of man to a behavioristic psychology which reduces man to a highly complex animal, or to a rigid determinism which reduces him to an intricate living machine, or to a viewpoint that considers all values, including moral values, to be a purely relative matter with no objective validity. It is obvious that the right thing to do must vary with the human situation, but this is quite different from saying that any individual or group can make a course of action right by deciding to have it so. However, within the areas of agreement mentioned above, there are large opportunities for the exponents of psychology and of religion to work together.

The most constructive approach appears to me to be that which Viktor Frankl calls "logotherapy," or the quest for life's meaning. The name need not be stressed; what it stands for is of vital importance. That it coheres with Christian presuppositions is evident from the fact that Robert C. Leslie's *Jesus and Logotherapy* is based on this point of view. My intention, however, is not to present or discuss a particular psychiatric system, or to try to say how to cure mental illness. Ours is the more limited objective of trying to suggest how a troubled but otherwise normal person can find reconciliation in the inner life.

Hostility is the attitude which most directly requires reconciliation. This is very common in our time, and it is likely to be directed against any person or group that impinges on us. The more immediate the relationship, as in the home or on the job, the more occasions for the hostility to crop out. Said Jesus, perhaps quoting Micah 7:6, "A man's foes will be those of his own household." (Matt. 10:36) He found it so when his mother and his brothers, thinking him mad, tried to put a stop to his ministry. It happens repeatedly—even in loving families, as we shall observe at greater length in the next chapter— it always has, and probably always will.

Linked with hostility are other attitudes of which the individual may be more conscious—anxiety, frustration, boredom, despair, adding up to the conviction that one amounts to nothing and that life is aimless and burdensome. One has both specific worries and a general state of uneasiness about the future. One tries to accomplish something, but seems to be getting nowhere. The dismay becomes chronic, and neither profanity nor drugs do much for the situation. If one gives up trying to do anything except what the routines of existence require, the whole enterprise of living seems senseless and an enormous ennui settles upon the soul. The medieval church called this the sin of *accidie*, or sloth, and while we no longer use the term, the condition is very much with us. All this creates a state of dull or acute unhappiness, the antithesis of peace of mind. For the religious person, it concels out the joy in the Lord which his faith promises him, and in a more pietistic day might lead one to believe he had committed the unpardonable sin. This is seldom heard of in our time, but the situation outlined in this paragraph besets great numbers of persons. It is so common that W. H. Auden has named our time the Age of Anxiety.

Various causes, or a combination of them, can bring about this state of mind and spirit. It can be a physical illness which eats away at one's nervous energy, or simply overtiredness. It can come from a sudden shock, as of grief at the loss of a loved one or a shattering disappointment. It can come from the self-centeredness which generates anger at the world for failure to accept and appreciate one. It can come from the more serious self-centeredness which is the essence of sin: the lovelessness which demands love without being willing to give it. It can come from a guilty conscience, though one may or may not be aware of a sense of guilt. It can come, as it often does in a highly competitive society, from being forced by his work or some other situation to do something against which his conscience or his inmost desire rebels.

In this situation, what is to be done about it? There is no panacea, but there are guidelines. Let us look at some of them.[6]

If one desires to emerge from such a disruptive or un-reconciled state of mind and spirit, the first requirement is the willingness to emerge. If one is consciously anxious or deeply depressed, he wants to get out of this unhappy state, so it looks like an easy requirement. Actually, it is not. In this situation, paralysis of the will may be the crux of the issue. Furthermore, one is apt to think that the trouble lies with other people or with the circumstances, not that he needs to do anything about it. And if he begins to see that he does, the requirements look too hard.

There is no sure way to arouse in another the willingness to seek, or even to accept, a new outlook on life. However, it can be greatly helped by acceptance of the other, in understanding friendliness, in loving concern that gets across barriers. In such an atmosphere, even unwelcome truth can be accepted without animosity; without this atmosphere of friendship, not simply assumed for the occasion but genuinely felt, no amount of advice is apt to produce much in the way of results except its rejection. But granted that such a climate of loving concern is present, every person must still make his own decision that he wants to make the effort toward a more meaningful and more inwardly satisfying life.

A second basic need is to locate and correct, if possible, any physical or social causes of the inner disturbance. It is only good sense that these be taken care of if they can be, whether by professional help or a more sensible regimen of life. One could say common sense, but it is not as common as it ought to be. Complex matters such as family tangles or economic insecurity or distasteful drudgery or racial tensions may not be readily removed, but in most cases something can be done in the right direction. Even a small alleviation gives new courage to hope for more. It is a function of the church to assist in this process, and for this reason the social outreach and challenge of the church must never be divorced from the inner health of the human spirit.

A third essential requirement for inner reconciliation is finding an object of love, loyalty, and devotion beyond one's self. It is essential to have such a human outreach; everybody needs somebody to love as well as to be loved by. The wider one's outreach in friendship, the greater the input which alleviates loneliness and emptiness. But is this all we need? The Christian faith finds an ultimate object of love and loyalty in God, our "Ultimate Concern" as Tillich calls this final object of devotion, or in Alfred North Whitehead's trenchant words, "Religion is the vision of something which stands beyond, behind, and within the passing flux of immediate things." [7] This is at least a part of what it means to love God "with all your heart, and with all your soul, and with all your mind, and with all your strength." Add to it the second great commandment, and it is clear why the supreme corrective of nervous fretting and inner alienation is to be found in Christian faith and action.

Whatever one thinks about religion, nobody can expect to get much release from his inner entanglements unless he projects himself outward beyond himself. Insight is important—it means to look within, and this we all need to do. If one believes in God as a guide to clearer vision, prayer is a great help in this respect. To prayer must be added one's best use of his mind to survey all the facts in any problem situation and look at its possibilities without prejudice. In other words, to insight must be added outlook. Yet insight and outlook together are not enough. To both must be added action with courage, wisdom, and love.

But what of self-love? This is a very prominent note in modern psychotherapy and counseling, with a frequent quoting of "love your neighbor as yourself" as evidence that Jesus assumed that one should love one's self. Much depends on the meaning attached to the term. If self-love means concern to be and to live at one's best, respecting one's own personality as one ought to respect that of every other person, seeking one's fullest creativity and most productive use of one's talents, this is indeed a good and necessary part of finding inner reconciliation. Too often it is taken to mean a self-concern which easily runs into self-centeredness. We may well believe that God desires all persons in his great human family to be happy, and happiness is a legitimate quest. But seeking one's own happiness at the cost of denying it to others is neither right nor is it often very effective.

Thus we come to the requirement for inner reconciliation which was alluded to earlier, the conviction that life has meaning. This cannot be conjured up at will; it may come along, perhaps unconsciously, as these other steps are taken. Yet it can be greatly aided by a Christian faith in God and a Christian understanding of man. Here let me quote a bit of my earlier writing:

> The Christian faith imparts meaning to life. A living faith that is centered in the God revealed in Christ takes our chaotic, disorganized selves, with their crude jumble of pleasures and pains, and knits them together into a steadiness and joy that can endure anything with God. The meaning of the cross is that sin can be forgiven, pain overcome, by the victory of God—a victory that is both within and beyond this earthly scene. The lives of countless Christians in this and every age bear witness to power through faith that in Christ we see what life is for.[8]

This sums it up as well as I could put it in brief compass. In one sense, the conviction that life has meaning is covered by everything else that has been said in this chapter. Yet it must be persistently and consistently spelled out, day by day and week after week in a great variety of ways, if the Christian message is to be relevant to man's inner needs. This leads to a brief concluding word.

The church and the "cure of souls"

The church has numerous functions to perform: the proclamation of the gospel message through preaching, the lifting of the people to God in worship, the challenging of the evils of society for the making of a more just and peaceful world, the transmission of the Christian heritage, the ministering to human need in any form in the name and the spirit of Christ.

The form of ministry most directly related to the theme of this chapter used to be called "the cure of souls." It is a good term; why not readopt it? In any case, it is a major function of the church. It extends throughout the total enterprise of a church, whether in worship, preaching the gospel message, pastoral counseling, the Christian fellowship, or the laymen's and the preacher's living and loving. In short, it is mediated through the most varied means of grace, not the sacraments only in the usual meaning of the term, but in many other sacramental experiences.

The grace of God for victory over suffering and the disclosure of its deeper meanings is mediated by the church not only through pastoral counseling but still more frequently through the ministry of the church as a supporting Christian fellowship. However latent this may be, it comes to the surface in times of deep trouble, as in serious illness, or the shattering bereavement and loneliness that death inevitably brings to those who love. Many years ago the late Willard Sperry wrote, "In response to some deep unreasoned prompting, men seek churches when life is most real." [9] This has been proved true again and again, and many readers of this book can validate it from their own experience more effectively than I could describe it.

It is not the minister only who is charged with "the cure of souls." We noted a procedure basic to either secular or religious counseling: the need of acceptance of the troubled person in loving understanding. In technical terms this may be called "unconditional positive regard" or "congruent empathetic understanding"; in more familiar Christian terms it means loving one's neighbor! Whether in the individual Christian family, or through friendly warmth in the local church, or through the spirit shown by its members in their community relations, the church can go—and does go—a long way toward mediating the grace of acceptance and bringing persons to fuller and richer living.

But what about sin? Is not the primary function of the church the conversion of sinners? Yes, in the sense that we all are sinners—in the churches and outside of them—and in ever-present need of newness of life in Christ. A type of evangelism which sets forth realistically the fact of sin and the availability of God's grace for the forgiveness of sin and transformation of life is very much in order. It should be loving and hope-inspiring, not lurid in its portrayal of the sinners' plight or based mainly on an appeal to fear. To be effective, it must induce self-awareness, self-criticism, and self-orientation. Granted that the power of God is at work within us to reshape motives, insights, and outlooks, his presence is an enabler but not a substitute for the human will. "God creates or reveals himself in man and man creates himself in God." [10]

We hear much in these days about how the lay people in the churches wish to be comforted rather than challenged. Certainly there needs to be a stirring of responsibility for the elimination of major social evils, and we may well rejoice that this note is being sounded. But is this any reason to disparage the ministry of comfort? Apparently Paul did not think so, for in the first chapter of II Corinthians he writes: "Blessed be the God and Father of our Lord Jesus Christ, the Father of mercies and God of all comfort, who comforts us in all our affliction, so that we may be able to comfort those who are in any affliction, with the comfort with which we ourselves are comforted by God." (II Cor. 1:3-4) And surely this is no mean service!

A great deal of the current criticism directed against the churches could be eliminated by a better knowledge, historical, theological and practical, of the mission of the church. With such knowledge one would be more apt to see it for what it is—a fallible human instrument but with a divine commission for carrying on Christ's work in the world. This work is many-sided. It ought to be done better, but it is being done. The church exists to be the carrier of the gospel of Christ to the inner lives of men and to the world. And since Christ is the light of the world—yesterday, today and forever—we need not fear that this light will be extinguished.

5. RECONCILIATION
THROUGH FRIENDSHIP

In this chapter we shall be dealing with reconciliation in interpersonal relations. In the usual meaning of the term as the bridging of rifts in interhuman relations, a distinction must be drawn between encounters of individual with individual, or within a small group personally known, and the vast impersonal structures of an increasingly complex society. The requirements of just treatment and of Christian concern apply in either relationship if we would have anything approximating a Christian society. Yet it is in person-to-person relations that reconciliation is most possible, and perhaps also most necessary.

Reconciliation in interpersonal relations is the more available because it is here that the more direct appeal can be made to heart, conscience, and knowledge of the situation and its probable consequences. Reinhold Niebuhr made this clear almost forty years ago in *Moral Man and Immoral Society* which has become a classic, with its thesis seldom disputed in the intervening years. However, it is often assumed that reconciliation in face-to-face situations is relatively inconsequential in view of the far-reaching injustices visited upon individuals by great centers of economic and political power. Granted that the latter must be viewed very seriously and challenged with more vigor than most Christians feel willing or able to muster, it is still true that reconciliation on a personal plane is vitally important. Without a reconstruction of personal attitudes among Christians toward those they know, there is unlikely to be much base for reaching out toward the vast unknown segments of society. "He who does not love his brother whom he has seen, cannot love God whom he has not seen." (I John 4: 20) Put "the world" in place of God in this statement, and it remains true.

The approach in this chapter will be made through an analysis of friendship and an application of the principles of friendship to some of the disturbing problems of our disordered society. Surprisingly enough, friendship—the *philia* which stands midway between *eros* and *agape* in Greek and New Testament concepts of love—has seldom been given serious and scholarly consideration. Friendship has been taken for granted, heralded repeatedly in song and story. Love is central to Christian theology and ethics, with *agape* lifted up and often contrasted with *eros*. But who writes on friendship? It is, of course, a common enough term with the assumption that everybody knows what it means. But do we?

This dearth of basic attention to friendship became evident to me when I came across a book dealing with it in a psychological context by Ignace Lapp, a French psychotherapist. Published as *Les Chemins de l'amitié* in 1964, it came out in English as *The Ways of Friendship* in 1966. This set me looking for other such analyses. All I could find was Emerson's *Essay on Friendship,* of unknown date but not less than a hundred years ago. There is, of course, Cicero's *De Amicitia* which along with his *De Senectute* I read in a special high school Latin class. I recall loving both, but whether they left any residue I cannot say.

There may be other books on friendship, but it is a much neglected subject in view of its central importance to human living. The subtitle of Fr. Lepp's book is "A Psychological Exploration of Man's Most Valuable Relationship." In view of the extent to which friendship, or the lack of it, permeates every other form of personal encounter, this appears to be a true judgment. Doubtless it is often subsumed under acquaintance, or in warmer terms under love, perhaps under the common psychological term of acceptance. Friendship has not only common elements with these terms but important differences. In my analysis I shall draw considerably on Fr. Lepp, less on the striking aphorisms of Emerson, but neither is mainly responsible for what follows.

An analysis of friendship

a. *The present situation.* Friendship is essentially a bridge from the aloneness of an individual to another human being, a form of outreach to and input from another with an emotional energy which affects the personality of both. From the stance of this preliminary definition, it is evident that the more complex and mobile the society, the more crowded, hurried, and harried the individuals within it, the harder it is to sustain deep and lasting friendships. Physical conjunction, as in the beehive apartments of great cities and the jostling of bodies in subways or commuter trains, banishes solitude but not loneliness. The emotions aroused are more likely to be those of annoyance than friendliness, and the crowded conditions of large cities leave many in the psychological aloneness which is the antithesis of the healing quiet of occasional solitude.

The rural community offers more occasions of neighborliness, and the author rejoices to have grown up in a country community where the people still have warm friendships, both with her and with each other.[1] It is a precious heritage, and the sustaining friendships that come to the fore in times of sickness and bereavement and the less poignant but heartwarming fellowship of the church supper ought not to pass from the current scene. Yet there are lonely people, and animosities generated by misunderstandings and unkind words, in the country as elsewhere. So it is in suburban society, where housewives sometimes visit about nothing in particular over the back fence or over their morning coffee, but also where people can live in the same block for years without knowing their neighbors' names. Add to such factors the rootlessness which comes from rapid transfers from place to place and the anonymity which comes from any number of sources, and it is not strange that friendship confronts barriers in our time.

These barriers are not only environmental and sociological but intellectual. In the writings of Jean-Paul Sartre, probably the ablest of the nonreligious existentialists of our time, a recurrent theme is the utter inability of man to break out of his inevitable solitude by encounter with others. Only by deluding himself by the banalities of daily life can he believe that he is not alone in a dark and cheerless world. This attitude of hopelessness toward anything deeper than the superficial enjoyments of life is widely reflected in the dramas and novels of our time. It is both cause and effect of a prevalent pessimism which often turns, not to companionship in deep friendships, but to superficial pleasures and to drugs as an anodyne of inner unhappiness.

The extensive consumption of drugs—by the young in the form of LSD, methedrine, and heroin, and by their elders as tranquilizers, alcohol, and the tobacco addiction—is related in no small measure to the lack of deep and rewarding friendships. On the surface it may appear that the drugs are taken because of the influence of friends and for the sake of social conformity. At a deeper level the reason they are taken is largely an attempt to escape from the hum-drum, uneasy, or stern realities of life which satisfying friendships could do much to alleviate or make endurable.

Thus it appears that of all the things which our troubled world now greatly needs, not the least of them is the healing, creative power of friendship. It is basic to every kind of constructive interpersonal relationship, and by such relationships to the total structure of society.

b. *What is friendship?* Friendship was defined earlier as the bridge from the aloneness of one individual to another in which there is an emotional energy which affects the personality of both. In other words, it is a mutual liking, based on some common interest or shared experience which draws the two together. It is the outreach of the total self-hood of one person toward that of another in reciprocity, though they remain different individuals who may have quite different interests, except at the point of meeting. A genuine friendship is able to transcend these differences and unite the two in an enriching communion of spirit.

Though I shall speak of friendship mainly in the relationship of one individual to another, it is obvious that there are often groups of friends. In fact, the Society of Friends nearly preempts the library listings under this heading! However, it is in the relationship of one person to another that groups of friends are formed.

What is the basis of the feeling which draws persons together and makes them friends, or to cite Emerson's fine phrase, gives us "inward irradiations"? The rapprochment may be sudden or gradual, and at least in the former case the cause may be difficult to define. To the degree that it is based on physical appearance, which figures far less in friendship than in erotic love, it is facial expression which gives some indication of inner spirit, rather than beauty, that is mainly responsible. To appearances are then added

80

words, which are a clearer index of attitudes, and apparently trivial but revealing acts.

Most friendships are of gradual rather than sudden formation. The discovery of a mutual interest usually makes the connection. It does not necessarily start from both sides at once; one may display an outgoing friendliness through words or some act of kindness which wins the response of the other. A friendship is both a subjective and an objective relation, and the object which brings the friends together will often determine the trend it takes. Yet the I-thou quality is never absent if the friendship survives, and friends must prize each other for what they are and not alone for what they have to offer.

Since friendship is an ambiguous term, often used too casually, its meaning may become clearer if we examine what it is not. It is not the same as acquaintance, even though the acquaintance may have interesting or attractive aspects. There is no friendship without some meeting— usually in person but quite possibly by correspondence— but many acquaintances do not become friendships in the true sense. The emotional dynamism is lacking or too diffused to merit the name.

Furthermore, friends are not the same as casual companions. Companions may play together in the same bowling or bridge club, or go out together for entertainment, and have an amicable relation which falls short of friendship. Even the gang, which may have a mischievous or a wholesome objective to unite it temporarily, usually has a shallow basis and a fluctuating membership. Fr. Lepp holds that no real friendship can be generated on the basis of pleasure only, for friendship requires a mutual interpenetration and deeper kinship of shared interests. Lacking these qualities, the relationship remains gregarious rather than being that of a community of persons.[2]

I believe this to be true. However, a recreational affinity may introduce persons to what can turn into a lasting friendship even though more than the introduction is required. As we shall observe later, within the family the ability and willingness of husband and wife and of parents and children to play together is often a much-needed cement to the friendly relations indispensable to a good home.

Not every common interest leads to friendship. It is possible to work together for years as colleagues in the same profession or as participants in a common cause and still not be friends. Friendship requires a sharing of experience, and the deeper the mutual interests and the richer the experiences in pursuit of them, the greater the potential for meaningful friendship. Yet the possibility of jealousy and petty bickering crops out even on the highest levels of endeavor. In any enterprise, sharp disagreement as to the right means to take to reach a common goal can disrupt a friendship. Appearances may then be kept up for public consumption or for the sake of diplomacy, but the spark has died.

But what of the relationship of friendship to acceptance and to love? Here the distinctions are less obvious, but they should be taken into account.

Friendship is not the same as acceptance in the psychological sense, for it implies a mutuality which acceptance often does not. When a psychotherapist deals so kindly and understandingly with his client that the latter now feels accepted and is encouraged to accept himself, there is no intention on the counselor's part that the two will now become fast friends. The client does not usually expect it, but when he does, the therapist must make it clear as kindly as possible that the relationship is temporary and professional. In ordinary personal relationships, to be accepted is very vital to happiness and effective living, but there is no guarantee that acceptance will lead to continuing personal friendships.

The most difficult distinction to draw is that between friendship and love, and it is probably for this reason that friendship has been so often subsumed under love in theological, ethical, and psychological discussions. Yet along with points of agreement, there are distinctions. Both are emotions which affect the total personality, and when rightly based and directed, very pleasurable and constructive emotions. Both relate persons to persons. Both are greatly needed, not only to be of service to others, but to meet the troubles of life and to live at one's best. Both call at times for much personal sacrifice. Yet they are not identical, and to assume that friendship is simply a milder or a more conventional form of love is to miss a distinctive meaning.

The distinction between friendship and erotic love is fairly clear, for the latter has a biological connection with the sex impulse which the former need not have. Friendship and erotic love may be found together, as they should be in a satisfying marriage; friendship as a relationship of spirit to spirit need have no such connection. What is usually called "Platonic love" between a man and a woman professes to be free from sexual desire but often is not. If the erotic element is really absent, as it can be in childhood or in maturity between persons sufficiently self-disciplined, it had better be called simply friendship.

But what of friendship and *agape*? Is not then friendship the equivalent of love? Almost, but not quite, and the New Testament fails to draw a clear distinction between *agape* and *philia*. Both are outgoing, self-giving, deeply concerned attitudes toward other persons—attitudes which generate the desire to be helpful in any way that is open. Yet there is an important difference. *Agape* need not be mutual; friendship must be. There is a great deal of unrequited love in the world, whether in the *eros* or *agape* sense; there is spurned friendship, but friendship does not exist if it is not returned.

The distinction is important, both theologically and practically. "In this is love, not that we loved God but that he loved us. . . ." (I John 4:10) God does not cease to love us when we fail to love him. We are bidden to love God supremely and the neighbor as ourselves; this, if taken seriously, calls for much loving of neighbor that may not be returned. In this respect *agape* makes higher demands than friendship. Yet if we are to reach the inner lives of others, both to help and to be helped by them, friendship is a necessary channel. *Agape* without personal friendship can render service, but it does not of itself create the mutual understanding which knits souls together. This is why services rendered from sincere motives of loving concern and active good will so easily slip over into the paternalism which offends the recipients. Both friendship and *agape* are essential to reconciliation.

c. *The requirements of friendship.* In view of these factors, how is a real friendship possible? That friendships are formed which bless our lives is certain. But how? Though it is not possible to form a friendship by rule or formula, any more than one falls in love by a set prescription, there are procedures which encourage, and others which stifle, friendship. Let us take a look at them.

A basic requirement is meeting. "All real living is meeting," said Martin Buber,[3] and before there can be any meeting of minds and hearts there must usually be a physical meeting. Though in rare instances such a meeting can occur by correspondence or some other form of connection,[4] to be in each other's presence and speak together is generally a prime requirement. Though we often cannot define the unconscious motivation that makes us feel drawn to some

84

persons more than to others, conversation and manner have much to do with it. In the conversation there is some disclosure of a common interest; the more significant the interest, the firmer the basis for friendship.

A second requirement is continuance of interchange by communication. This does not necessarily mean much talk. Whether this is possible or desirable depends on the circumstances. Those thrown together by living conditions, propinquity of work, or a common cause had better feel free to talk together. Both too much reserve and too much aimless chatter are barriers to friendship. This is not to say that one must converse only on lofty themes. Said Koheleth, "For everything there is a season, and a time for every matter under heaven" (Eccles. 3:1), and there is a time for small talk as well as for serious conversation. Yet communication there must be. Even though it may be on controversial subjects on which there may be a radical difference of opinion, it must be in mutual respect.

Friends who are separated by long distances are often too busy in our time to write frequently. As a consequence they "get out of touch," a common term with a true meaning, for it is the touch of life with life which both generates friendships and keeps them warm and living. The exchange of Christmas greetings with a bit of news and even a brief personal note is more than a social custom; it is a lifesaver for many friendships.

Friendship requires generosity. This does not always involve tangible gifts, though there is a place for this when it is not overdone with the subconscious motive of attempting to purchase another's friendship. The generosity that is required is openness of spirit, the willingness to make one's self available to another. Many feel themselves friendless and lonely, even to the point of neurosis and a warped personality, because they have been unwilling or unable to crawl out of their reserve into the sunlight of good fellowship. Whether or not this condition may require psychotherapy, it requires self-confidence and conquest of the self-love which is in reality self-centeredness. Emerson put it simply but truly when he wrote, "The only way to have a friend is to be one."

A friend must be willing to receive as well as to give. This means openness to receive the friendship of another, but also the willingness to receive services and even tangible gifts if they are within reason. If one party can do more than the other in such giving, there should be no embarrassment in receiving. Friendship must never succumb to the temptation of becoming barter.

Friendship requires sacrifice, not in the sense of a conscious martyrdom, but the frequent surrender of one's desires for the sake of another. In brief, no selfish friendship survives. The quickest way to kill a friendship is for one of the parties to feel that he is being made the tool of the other's whim or quest for self-aggrandizement. This is to say that there must be complete sincerity in self-giving. At this point friendship comes very close to *agape*.

Attention has been called to the importance of mutual respect and the right of friends to differ in their beliefs and concerns, so long as there is a common center. Many friendships, and marriages as well, are wrecked by a dictatorial attitude. Ridicule or scorn of another's beliefs and interests, even though they may seem like silly or outlandish notions, is not the way to preserve friendship. There may be a need to try to change certain attitudes, but for one adult to dominate another is to jeopardize their friendship. Dangerous also is an abject compliance. To quote Emerson again, "I am equally balked by antagonism and by compliance. I hate, where I looked for a manly resistance, to find a mush of concession. Better be a nettle in the side of your friend than his echo."

This leads to a very important aspect of friendship: its potential universality. Warm, deep, and lasting friendships can be formed between persons of any race or color, any nation, any social class, rich and poor, young and old, children and adults, employer and employed, highly educated and illiterate, teacher and student, man and woman. It is obvious that many friendships are formed between men and other men and by women with other women. It is unfortunate that society is often too quick to suspect homosexuality in such instances. But what it is important to emphasize at this point is friendship's potential universality.

Note that it is *potential* universality, for Christ as the Son and Revealer of God is the only fully universal friend. Jesus had particular friendships, of whom we know most about the twelve disciples, Lazarus and his sisters Mary and Martha, and Mary Magdalene. John appears to have been Jesus' closest friend, and it must have grieved Jesus greatly when his friend Judas betrayed him. He shocked his contemporaries by having friends among drunkards, tax collectors and sinners, and probably also by his going against custom in his friendships with women. Yet as the living Christ he speaks to his followers today as to the Twelve at their last supper together, "You are my friends if you do what I command you." (John 15:14)

No one of us in our finiteness can have an unlimited body of friends, though we may have a wealth of friends, which is one of life's greatest treasures. Not only are we limited by time and space and the possibility of personal contacts, but our meeting of minds and spirits is limited also by individual interests and our "inward irradiations." This situation must be accepted without rebellion, though not prematurely or until we have gone as far as we can in the outreach of spirit to spirit.

It is within these limits, not in some impossible beyond, that both the possibilities and the problems of interpersonal relations are found. How friendship is related to reconciliation within these relations must be our inquiry in the remainder of the chapter.

Marriage and the family

We shall look now at some areas of interpersonal relations in which friendship is greatly needed, but in which hostility too often prevails. In none of these will the author attempt to cover every aspect of the question. For example, in the field of marriage counseling, any number of excellent books and articles are available and it would be inappropriate for one who has never married to try to supplement them. Nevertheless, a great many marriages go on the rocks and end in divorce or mutual bitterness for lack of what has been discussed thus far: a wholesome and constructive friendship. Let us examine the reasons as a clue to reconciliation in this area.

A stable marriage requires both sexual attraction and a deeper and more spiritual form of love which results in lasting loyalty and fidelity; in short, both *eros* and *agape*. But must it not have *philia* as well? If what has been said earlier in this chapter is true, it must.

Erotic love is by nature far less stable than friendship, for it depends more on physical attraction and sexual response. Fr. Lepp says that misunderstandings between husband and wife and a consequent breakup of the marriage relationship is due far more often to a lack of communication of minds and spirits than to sexual incompatibility.[5] Erotic love is fragile; when beauty fades, or quarrels arise, or familiarity dulls the keenness of attraction, sexual enjoyment is no longer sufficient to sustain the union. Friendship, on the other hand, if it is genuine and deeply rooted, can survive all these hazards plus those of old age, illness, and radical shifts in temporal fortunes. When marriage vows are taken "to have and to hold, from this day forward, for better, for worse, for richer, for poorer, in sickness and in health, to love and to cherish, till death us do part, according to God's holy ordinance," much more is involved than sexual affinity.

Why have such vows? In our present state of easy divorce, premarital intercourse, and even of the undisguised living together and bearing children by prominent figures in the entertainment world, is marriage necessary? The answer is found not only in social custom and the need of legal stability, though these are important, but in human nature itself. A "free love" arrangement is almost inevitably transient, and because of its transiency hazardous. In the early days of the Communist regime in Russia, free love was widely advocated, but it simply did not work. The preservation of a stable Soviet society required the subjection of marital unions to laws and regulations.

Attention was called in the preceding chapter to the fact that hostility is a very common attitude within the family. This is not new in the world's history, for the book of Proverbs has this to say of it:

> It is better to live in a corner of the housetop
> than in a house shared with a contentious woman.
> (21: 9; also 25: 24)

Elsewhere the figure of speech is changed a bit but the meaning stands:

> It is better to live in a desert land
> than with a contentious and fretful woman.
> (21:19)

89

Why the woman? Because the passage was doubtless written by a man.

But why the contention? In part, this is due to the fact that judgments formed in the period of passionate love are apt to be warped. The ugly then appears beautiful; perversity is interpreted as strength; silly talk appears to the lover as sparking wit. Within the close juxtaposition of married life, the illusion wears off. Along with this common phenomenon, the strains of the family situation inevitably induce tensions which it takes considerable effort to surmount. Even though "the two shall become one flesh" (Matt. 19:5 N.E.B.), they remain two individuals with two dispositions. Differences of opinion about the care of the house or the children, the work or other duties of each, what to do for recreation and whether it is to be done together or separately, disagreements on money matters or on politics, religion or each other's friends, and a thousand little things which become major by their accumulation—all these place an inevitable strain on the bonds of love. "Mental cruelty," which is usually not intentional cruelty but a cruel state of affairs from failure to adjust to these strains, is the result.

In this situation there must be something strong enough to surmount the tensions, or the marriage breaks up. This something is love. But love which is deep and lasting also must have in it the qualities of friendship.

A glance at the requirements of friendship as stated earlier makes evident how the lack of them leads to tragic consequences. A stable and satisfying friendship requires mutual interests and shared experiences; there must be meeting and communication. There must be a generous self-giving, with the giving and receiving of what one has to share. Friendship requires sacrifice. It calls for mutual respect and the right to differ in beliefs and opinions, with neither dominance nor abject concession on either side.

It must avoid jealousy because friendship by its very nature is inclusive, and it can be formed across the most diverse human groups so long as there is a meeting of hearts and minds.

These qualities of friendship characterize marriage at its best. When the two partners have very little in common except a transient sexual attraction, no meeting of minds and even little communication unless it be in harsh words, no willingness to sacrifice or to give to the other except in a grudging spirit, no respect for the other's selfhood and legitimate range of differences in thought and daily activities—when the union has reached this state, the marriage is about over. The parties may stay together for prudential reasons or for the children's sake. Sometimes this is the one bond of union, though jealousy for their affection or quarreling over their care and upbringing may also be a bone of contention. Yet the marriage as such is severed.

But is not jealousy indigenous to marriage? And must not friendship within marriage be exclusive rather than inclusive? Here the answer must be both yes and no with a careful differentiation of terms. That part of the marriage ceremony which requires assent to the pledge, "forsaking all others, keep thee only unto him so long as ye both shall live" belongs there. There cannot be promiscuity in marriage, either sexual or spiritual, and still keep the marriage lasting and firm. Yet this does not preclude either party from having friends, both of the same and of the opposite sex, if these relationships are disciplined to the point of not becoming rivals to the marriage. The more open and aboveboard the friendships, the less dangerous; the disruption comes from secret meetings and hidden activities that one is not free to talk about with one's spouse. An oversuspicious jealousy breaks the marriage tie, but so does too much complaisance about infidelity.

Thus it appears that in the present fragile state of domestic relations in our society, friendship has much to offer to the marriage relationship. Though it is difficult to generate for the sake of overcoming a rift when the break has occurred, it is not impossible. If a friendship once broken is to be mended, it takes effort rooted in self-denial, subordination of personal ego, communication with the difficult task of seeing through each other's eyes, great patience, and the best of wisdom one can muster as to his words and acts. A counselor can shed light on the situation, but the two individuals must work it out together. *It can be done,* and the friendship thus recovered or engendered is the most stable basis for reconciliation.

Another procedure is much less difficult and much more satisfying. This is to enter into marriage with the friendship already formed and never let it flag, but grow in richness and depth. When *eros, agape,* and *philia* meet, the family is secure and its joy is boundless.

The generation gap

In the preceding section little was said about children. Yet they are very important to the stability and joy of the family. There should not be too many of them, but those who come into the world should have the loving care of both parents. Both should participate unitedly in the forms of discipline which are essential to the children's personal growth. Furthermore, though the present generation gap is usually assumed to connote the behavior and attitudes of teenage youth and young adults, what precedes this period is much related to it.

Most parents love their children, but it does not follow that they always learn to be friends with them. In former days there was probably too much authoritarian repression. Children were told what they must do and how to behave, and they were punished for disobedience. Under penalty of a severe scolding, if not spanking, children were forbidden to talk back to their elders. Sometimes such coercive measures resulted in alienation and hostility, a smarting sense of injustice, and a repression of the children's personality and initiative.

All this is changed. A spirit of permissiveness pervades most homes. Children do very much as they please, sometime scolded but not with a note of authority that commands respect. At a young age they learn to defy their parents and get what they want, if indeed it is not given to them without such defiance. The language children often use toward their parents, thereby proving themselves the masters, would have been utterly shocking to an earlier generation.

The first and older procedure was wrong because it was too authoritarian. It cultivated discipline but not always self-discipline. The second is wrong because it fails to develop respect for legitimate authority and either discipline or self-discipline. To be fruitful, discipline requires a gradual growth in both freedom and restraint, the latter becoming increasingly inward as one accepts the limitations imposed by the society around him and by an emerging sense of right and wrong. Children today to an alarming degree grow up with a premature freedom in which there is little restraint except the demands imposed by conformity to the peer group, which quite probably is itself exercising an undisciplined freedom.

Such permissiveness in childhood is not the only reason children so often break with their parents in adolescence, but it is an important factor. Linked with it today is the fact that few children, especially in urban society, have much to do except go to school, play, and watch television. The chores of an earlier day have been banished by social change and the laborsaving devices spawned by technology, and gregarious activities have taken the place of household duties. The result is a gain in some respects, notably in better schools than formerly, but also a loss in personal responsibility.

We cannot turn back the tide of history. Nevertheless, responsible cooperation within the family needs to be cultivated. Note was taken earlier that families need to play together. Even if there is not much work in which the young can cooperate, this can go far toward cementing friendship. Family outings are indispensable. In the Christian family, a common relationship to the church does much for the family as well as for the church.

Family members must communicate if they are to be drawn together. Each should be free to talk of the concerns that interest him and receive a respectful hearing. The family dinner—often the only meal when all eat together, if they do then—should be a time of interesting conversation in the sharing of the day's experiences. Too often, it is a time of silent, if not glum, ingestion of food. And if it is to be a really Christian family, it had better begin with the saying of grace as at least a momentary recognition of God's presence.

To look now at the current adolescent and student rebellion and the so-called generation gap, much of it is understandable, even though at points regrettable. It is not all bad, but the adverse side of it may stem largely from the lack of family friendship in the previous years. This is not to say that it is entirely the parents' fault. The present social climate as well as the natural impulse of the adolescent to cast off restraint is favorable to it. Some adolescents reared in good homes with the best of advantages treat their parents, school administrators, and other adult leaders cruelly and with an insensitivity far removed from the "love" of which they are prone to talk. Some repudiate the Establishment with apparently no thought of what they owe to it culturally, financially, and personally. Some harm themselves by taking to premarital sex and to drugs as if this were a right long denied them, as victims of an unkind world now set free. In these demands for freedom, and especially in regard to drugs, which too often do irreparable damage to their bodies and to their future personhood, their families are deeply troubled. Then frustration and tension on both sides, if not outright separation, is likely to ensue.

Nevertheless, a number of things must be taken into account before judging the young too harshly. The first is that beards and sideburns, long hair and fantastic clothes do not make the man, and will pass as all fads do. A second observation is that the young abhor hypocrisy, and if they take to illicit sex and drugs, they have plenty of examples in the loose marriage ties, hidden adulteries, and consumption of alcohol and amphetamines by their elders. A third is that the erotic stimuli poured out by the mass media for the past twenty years or more, and the violence on which as children they were reared by television and war toys, could scarcely fail to leave their effects. Added to newly burgeoning sexual feelings and the desire for power, the present situation has social causes. A fourth thing to remember, and perhaps the most important, is that with all its crudity, which often runs into obscenity, there is much that is good in the protests of the young in our time.

From observations based on my years of teaching in two colleges and two theological seminaries, I believe that, on the whole, the youth of today are more serious-minded than their predecessors. This judgment does not apply to the hippies, who seem conspicuously lacking in a sense of social responsibility, being interested chiefly in sexual liberty and defiance of the Establishment with little concern for the feelings of their parents or the rights of the public. But not all young people, or even all those who decry the Establishment and want to see it changed, are hippies.

The great mass of students across the land are in school to get an education, and they work hard at this enterprise. A demonstration, though it may seem massive, seldom enlists more than a small minority of the student body and is often joined by others who are not students. They are more mature, both intellectually and socially than earlier student generations. At the same time, they want an education more directly geared than formerly to the world in which they must live, and they do not hesitate to make this desire known.

The young of today want a world in which war will be abolished, and in great numbers they rebel against the immorality, injustice, and cruel destructiveness of the war in Vietnam. Some of this protest is doubtless based on a natural desire not to be killed or maimed for life, and violence occasionally breaks out in the demonstrations. Most of it roots in their aversion to the folly and barbarity of war, a point of view which many of us who are older have long held. The demonstrations are very largely nonviolent, with the skirmishes with the police sometimes played up out of true proportion.

The youth want also equality and justice for the black and brown minorities and for the poor. Many are eager to join the Peace Corps or VISTA for constructive service, and more than a few of them are to be found tutoring ghetto children, serving in black youth centers, or aiding in voter registration. Of late, since the environment has become such a central concern, they are demanding its protection from pollution. This may prove to be a mediating interest with their elders.

In behalf of such causes as these the young demonstrate, hold their teach-ins, sometimes seize buildings and defy authority. One need not approve all that is done in such matters, either by the youth or the police, to believe that the heart of today's youth is sound and that their concern for a more man-centered, less money-centered world is profoundly reasonable.

The church

The reader may be wondering why so little has been said in this chapter about the Christian gospel or the church as its carrier. The omission is deliberate, for friendship is no private domain of Christianity. Friendship as a primary agent of reconciliation can exist within or outside of it, with or without a religious foundation. To claim it as the exclusive prerogative of Christians would be to fly in the face of obvious facts.

Nevertheless, the churches have a great responsibility in the matter. It will be appropriate to close this chapter by suggesting some of them.

The encouragement of friendship through a mutually related and supporting fellowship is not the only mission of the church, but it is a very important one. When the atmosphere of a church lacks warmth of friendship among its members they are prone to cease attending, for the love of God, unless mediated through a human agency, seems formless and remote. When a church is socially or racially stratified, and its members seek fellowship only with "our kind of folks," it lacks the universality which both *philia* and *agape* call for. The complaints against the churches on this account are sometimes overdone, for since the church is an institution of society it is inevitably to some degree affected by the prevailing culture of its members. Yet the church as the Body of Christ is by nature a supraracial, supranational, supraeducational, supraclass body. If any person that desires to be a follower of Christ fails to feel at home in it, something is wrong that cries out for correction.

An alarming situation today is the exit of the young from its portals. Much is being done to try to attract them and the more secular-oriented of their elders by new forms of worship. Certainly the church must adapt its mode of conveying the gospel message to the times, and some of these departures from tradition have the basic requirements of worship: reverence, dignity, and fitness. Others seem more like raucous dissonance designed for entertainment rather than worship. On this, no lasting Christian foundations can be built.

A more serious situation tends to alienate the young and some of their elders. When a congregation is dominated by a power structure, often consisting of conservative members of the Establishment who have little sympathy with the interests and attitudes of contemporary youth, the young tend to walk out. They then seek their religious refreshment in their own forms of worship or in mystical meditation, with or without drugs. That they would blend this with their activism is an indication that the young people of our time are by no means irreligious. There is a burst of interest today in the Eastern religions, such as Zen Buddhism, and in seeking the leadership of Hindu gurus. This may be a passing fad, but it is indicative both of a religious hunger and of the failure of the the churches to satisfy it.

A further bearing of the theme of this chapter is the imperative need of the church to set its own house in order. It was stated earlier that interest in a common cause does not guarantee friendship. This appears in its most distressing form when there are animosities and bickerings within churches. This situation may appear in a gulf between clergy and laymen, or between groups of lay people who have radically different ideas as to what the church should be doing and how it should be run. Cleavages sometimes center around particular leaders, sometimes around clashing issues, but in either case friendships are strained and the church is weakened in its mission. The presence of this spirit in local churches is more than a little responsible for the flight of so many of the younger clergy to other forms of service. A deeper and more Christlike spirit might not settle all the problems, but it would afford a firmer ground for their settlement.

The rift most difficult to bridge, whether in a local congregation or a denomination, is the disparity between the conservative and the liberal points of view. This cleavage may exist around either theology or social action, usually, though not always, in conjunction. The conservative feels that the liberal has rejected the fundamentals of the faith (hence the term fundamentalist) and is undermining the foundations of a stable society. The liberal thinks that the conservative is blocking progress toward a fuller apprehension of the truth and a more just society, such as the gospel imperatives require. Differences in attitude and opinion too often turn into personal ill will, and the effectiveness of the church suffers from dissension.

There is no panacea for overcoming this situation. However, in addition to the guidelines for the Christian in controversy suggested in the last chapter of this book, some other things may be said. The first is the need to realize that friends may differ, even on important issues, and still remain friends if there is some deep common bond. This bond ought to be loyalty to Christ, to the gospel of love which Christ enjoins, and to the church, which is its carrier. A second requirement is the need to understand why the exponent of the opposite point of view thinks as he does. Everybody's conscience is shaped by his parental background, his environment—whether past or present—and that which in his own experience has seemed most vital to his needs. One man may find this directive in biblical literalism and the social *status quo;* another in fresh openings and new ways of thinking. It should still be possible to differ in Christian love.

Whether or not friendship is to be judged "man's most valuable relationship," it is still indispensable to the reconciliation of person to person in impinging relations. How it must be supplemented by justice will be our concern in the next chapter.

6. RECONCILIATION THROUGH JUSTICE

We move now to the consideration of that aspect of the social order in which the deepest tensions are found, most difficult to bridge, and most dangerous to society as a whole when the bridges of understanding remain unbuilt. This is the sphere of major groups within which it is impossible to know large numbers of individuals. What individual persons do affects, and often affects very deeply, the lives of other individuals within these groups, but the limitations of human existence preclude having, to any great extent, a person-to-person encounter.

These areas include relations between the nations, the races, the employer and employed in major industries and various other forms of economic life, the sexes when considered mainly in distinction from each other, political parties when viewed collectively, and much else that is important to contemporary society. In these fields, justice is the primary principle through which reconciliation must be brought about if it is to be attained.

All civilized societies are concerned about justice, and have laws, courts, and both juridical and penal systems in the attempt to secure and preserve it. In a democracy, these figure much more largely than in a totalitarian regime, but even there is found a semblance of preserving justice, or the regime could not exist. In no society are the restraints on injustice which the laws and courts aim at fully effective. As a result the victims of injustice are bound to feel hostility toward their oppressors. Herein lies the marvel of Jesus' words from the cross, "Father, forgive them, for they know not what they do."

The line between person-to-person and major-group-to-major-group relations cannot be sharply drawn. For example, this is very evident in the race question, where excellent civil rights laws have been passed, but tensions and hostile attitudes remain which prevent the laws' full and harmonious observance. Here, as in the women's liberation movement, the law offers more leeway than social prejudice permits, and just attitudes between individuals are as vital to reconciliation as are the laws. So, we shall not leave behind in this chapter what was said in the previous one.

Some observations on justice

a. *What is justice?* Unlike the situation in regard to friendship, justice has been discussed and analyzed times without number, from the time of Hammurabi in ancient Babylon and of Socrates, Plato, and Aristotle in Greece to the present. A large part of the course of civilization in general and of ethical principles and rules of conduct in particular have centerd at this point. Even the most primitive societies, and small children today, have an elemental sense of fair play which cannot be infringed upon without upsetting social harmony and arousing hostility on one or both sides of the question.

Despite this major attention to justice, it is not an easy term to define. Its classic definition, coming down from Aristotle, is "giving to every man his due." Yet it is by no means self-evident what is "due" in every instance. Justice clearly has to do with the securing of rights to those who would otherwise be denied them. Yet there is seldom full agreement as to what these rights are. The oppressor and the oppressed, actuated by self-interest, have a difference of opinion at this point, and even the impartial observer may find it difficult to decide among competing claims. "Circumstances alter cases," and the rights to which one may be justly entitled often depends on a complex network of circumstances. This is why we have the U.S. Constitution and the Supreme Court for its interpretation as a final arbiter in disputed issues. But even so, these nine men are human and finite.

The Declaration of Independence states that all men "are endowed by their Creator with certain unalienable rights, that among these are Life, Liberty and the pursuit of Happiness." Though this is true and very important, grave questions remain. If life is always to be preserved, what of killing in war, in capital punishment, in police action, in self-defense, to say nothing of permitting death by hunger and malnutrition? If liberty is an inalienable right, where draw the line between the legitimate freedoms of speech, worship, assembly and dissent, and anarchy? This is no small issue today. Happiness is something everybody ought to have, but at what points does the happiness of some limit that of others?

Without attempting to give an impregnable definition of justice, it may tentatively be defined as that situation in human society in which the welfare of all persons and the conditions essential to their creative and satisfying living are most fully assured. This differs from Jeremy Bentham's famous formula "the greatest good of the greatest number," in that the criterion is qualitative rather than numerical, and it requires the taking into account of all persons, however diverse their situations. Since every person is beloved of God and is of intrinsic worth, every person—whether known or unknown—ought to be of concern to the rest of humanity. When any person or group is mistreated and basic rights are denied, the injustice should disturb us all. Said John Donne, "Ask not for whom the bell tolls; it tolls for thee."

In every system of justice, there must be both freedoms and restraints. The restraints must be imposed both from within in self-control and from without where self-discipline is not sufficient to protect the general welfare. In an ideally just society, every individual would live at his best in harmonious relations with all those whose lives touch his. There is no ideally just society, and it seems improbable that there ever will be while sin remains to prompt some men to seek possessions or power at the expense of others. Yet every society can be more just than it is, and it is the imperative of Christian love to make it so.

b. *Justice and love.* A problem closely connected with the meaning of justice is its relation to love. This is a special problem for Christian ethics because, while the records indicate that Jesus said much about love, he appears to have said almost nothing about justice. In fact, he seems to have been little concerned about the State, the economic order, the penal system, the restraint of evildoers by law or of aggressive nations by force. This may have been the better for us, because Christians, like others, must discover what they regard as just amid changing social conditions, and a set of fixed rules, if literalized, might have brought havoc instead of good. Yet in the Christian perspective, justice must not be divorced from love. When love in the Christian sense is understood to include vast groups of persons, the far-away neighbor as well as the near, then justice is the instrument through which love finds expression.

But is love possible without a personal relationship? And is not justice of necessity impersonal? Both *eros* and *philia* require personal encounter, but the neighbor-love at the heart of Christian ethics need not be so regarded. The love of neighbor means active good will, concern for the welfare of others, eagerness to be helpful in any way that is open. As such, it is an emotion which ought to actuate us strongly, even to the point of the sacrificial self-giving of which the cross is the symbol. But neighbor-love is not a passionate sentiment that requires a meeting of person with person and of heart with heart. In its most exacting form, it is self-giving without the reciprocity implicit in such meeting. It is personal in the sense of being directed toward persons, even the unseen and unknown. Justice is personal in this sense when it becomes the instrument of love. Yet in neither is individual acquaintance a prerequisite.

Some writers on Christian social ethics, notably Emil Brunner in his classic *Justice and the Social Order,* differentiate sharply between justice and love. Brunner holds that justice is impersonal, a "sense of things fixed," while love is warmly personal. He recognizes that justice changes with changing circumstances, yet holds that it is concerned, not with the individual as such, but with his rights in relation to the world of systems.[1] This impersonal stance is often assumed to be needed for an impartial justice, and it is of some significance that the classic symbol of justice is a blindfolded woman holding evenly balanced scales. This concept of justice omits love. From this position I must register dissent.

Thus far I have tried to give an affirmative interpretation of the meaning of justice. Yet one very common understanding of it must be emphatically rejected. This is the idea that giving everyone his due means "getting even," retaliating, doing as one has been done to. This conception seems to be ingrained in human nature, and is found in the blood revenge of both primitive and advanced societies, the *lex talionis* ("an eye for an eye and a tooth for a tooth"), which Jesus repudiated, and the common assumption in today's world that the purpose of punishment for crime is retribution. Not only does this principle run counter to Christian love, but it is not even sensible. As we should have learned from centuries of experience but apparently have not, retaliation breeds counter–retaliation, hostilities become deeper and more dangerous, and violence, whether of angry words or the colossal destruction of life and property in war, begets more violence in an endless chain of evil consequences.

c. *The requirements of justice.* What, then, must be present if we are to have a form of social justice which is the instrument of love, but without the necessity of face-to-face encounter? Certain conditions must be met if we are to have a more just society, such as Christian love calls for and which we must have if reconciliation among discordant groups is ever to be brought about.

The first of these requirements is love in the sense defined above—a genuine concern for persons because they are persons, respect for their personhood, a desire to see their highest well-being assured, willingness to act toward this end and to give one's self at personal cost. This is altruism, but in a Christian context it goes deeper than altruism. Neighbor-love requires personal commitment, regardless of whether the persons to whom the commitment is made are personally known. With it belongs a sense of social responsibility, which means an imperative to act for the neighbor's good in any feasible way that is open.

Such love mingled with justice is not new in Christian history, though it has often been called simply service. It has been present from the beginning of the church in its

106

care for the weak, the helpless, the sick, the poor, the victims of other men's oppression. It came to a vigor often underestimated and sometimes disparaged in the social gospel movement of the earlier half of the twentieth century. It is present today under new forms amid altered circumstances.

A second requirement is intelligent analysis of the situation, knowledge of the facts, clear-seeing judgment of the circumstances and of the most feasible methods of changing them for the better. In projects calling for action, one must look before he leaps. Compromise of procedure with the differing views of others may be called for, but not the surrender of basic conviction. Progress in most areas of long-standing injustice comes slowly; it is seldom possible to move immediately from where we are to where we ought to be. Gradualism may be tolerated as an antidote to precipitate action, but not as a stalling process or substitute for action.

A third requirement is that an individual must work with others to accomplish much, and often with many others through structures that have power. This is why most major changes require political action, and frequently economic foundations as well. It is to deny a basic part of the expression of Christian love to say that churches should "keep out of politics." To "stick to the gospel" is to present information and encourage the motivation that leads to just and constructive action of every kind. Though it is usually injudicious for the church as an organized body to espouse a particular political party, the issues are manifold which require legal action, and laws are made or changed through political action. That is what government is, and Plato's word that the penalty for lack of participation by the good is to be ruled by evil men still holds true. Aristotle, though not entirely democratic in his own views, spoke truth when he said, "If liberty and equality, as is thought by some, are chiefly to be found in democracy, they will be best attained when all persons alike share in the government to the utmost." [2]

A basic requirement of justice is this combination of liberty and equality which a democracy seeks to promote. Liberty must have limits placed upon it for the general good, but a freedom inherent in the dignity of personhood is essential to any just society. It is not literally true that "all men are created equal," either in bodily or mental vigor or environmental opportunities. Yet justice requires that all should have equality of opportunity according to their ability to use it, and all should have equal rewards for equal services. It is obvious that at both of these points we are still a long way from justice in what professes to be our democratic society.

Liberté, egalité, fraternité—these were the watchwords of the French Revolution. However much they were snowed under in that event by the desire for power, it would be hard to find a more succinct or accurate summing up of the requirements of justice. Had Aristotle added brotherhood to liberty and equality, he would have had a more complete statement of true democracy. Brotherhood is the secular correlate of Christian love, and both are greatly needed if that justice is to be obtained which is the presupposition of reconciliation in major social groups.

Race and black power

The racial situation in the United States is one of enormous complexity. Many books have been written upon it, which might be a sufficient reason for omitting it from this one. Yet in the domestic scene it is the point at which reconciliation is most urgent, and in which personal attitudes are most deeply divided. Only the war in Vietnam surpasses it in peril or divisiveness, and the two are closely bound together.

Far from attempting to cover the entire picture, I propose in this section first to review in outline how we came to the present situation. Then I shall try to say what I think could and should be done by churches and Christian citizens who desire to become agents of reconciliation.

The black man in America has been the victim of injustice ever since his ancestors were torn from their homes in Africa and brought as slaves to this country more than three hundred years ago. The nature of these injustices is too familiar to require retelling. Slavery was accepted in the South for economic reasons, which soon became cultural and psychological ones as well. The North, not needing slave labor, condemned slavery but accepted segregation. The Civil War ended slavery but not cultural serfdom, and segregation continued in both areas, in the churches as elsewhere in the surrounding culture.

In both South and North the idea was prevalent that Negroes were of an inferior race. This was nurtured by the fact that lack of educational opportunities, economic subsistence, and proper living conditions created a vicious circle which so perpetuated the idea of inferiority that the Negroes themselves absorbed it. This negative self-image stifled effort to improve and made the situation worse. However, there were some redeeming features. The blacks were deeply religious, finding in their faith the power to endure their lot and creating by their spirituals the only truly indigenous American folk music. There were Christian people and other concerned persons, both Northerners and Southerners, who gave their money to establish Negro schools and colleges, and the favored few were thus able somewhat to surmount the limiting conditions of their environment.

In 1896 a historic Supreme Court decision, *Plessy vs. Ferguson*, established the principle of "separate but equal" public facilities, which included the public schools. Though at the time it seemed a step forward, it clinched the existing practice of segregation. As all know, this was reversed by another Supreme Court decision in 1954, but the end is not yet.

In the first half of the twentieth century, more and more Negro young people became educated and entered the professions as doctors, lawyers, teachers, and scientists, or made their mark in the arts as writers and musicians. They won respect for their achievements, but still had to fight social barriers, and their success left the great mass of the Negro poor untouched.

During this same period, which was at the height of the liberal social gospel movement in the churches, a good many ministers and other leaders became keenly aware of the need of racial justice, and tried to further it. However, this failed to penetrate far enough into the local congregations to bring about much action from them. In the North the churches were usually officially open to persons of all races but segregated by social pressures and middle-class cultural homogeneity; in the South the segregation was complete. How permeating this situation was is evidenced by the fact that in 1939, the union of three Methodist churches—two of them severed over the slavery issue in 1844—was accomplished only by placing Negro members in a separate unit called the Central Jurisdiction while whites were geographically distributed. This was eradicated in 1968 in the union with the Evangelical-United Brethren Church, but its traces remain in certain still-segregated annual conferences.

Soon after the first World War a movement began which has continued and is very crucial to the present situation,

This was the movement of Negroes to northern cities in the hope of higher incomes, accentuated by the loss of employment in the South through technological advances in agriculture. They found better pay, but this was still inferior to that of white workers and their unemployment rate was—and still is—much higher. As they moved into the cheapest living quarters available, their white neighbors moved out and the Negro ghetto was created. Today with its substandard housing, inferior schools, inadequate employment and recreational facilities, rats and roaches, the ghetto is the basic key to the smarting injustice of the black situation.

In the 1950's, barriers began to be broken down with the setting aside of the "separate but equal" provision by the Supreme Court, but the desegregation of the schools was slow and obstacles remained in the crucial areas of housing and employment. In the 1960's with the emergence of the charismatic, nonviolent Christian leadership of Martin Luther King, Jr., the work of the NAACP and the Urban League, and the political action of many concerned white persons, the Civil Rights Bill was passed in 1964 and the Voting Rights Act in 1965. These were watersheds which gave great hope, and they did go far to open up opportunities, especially in voting, which had long been denied.

However, the optimism did not last long. With a new sense of their own identity, the blacks began to demand that other long-standing injustices be cast off. What has happened since in the way of declarations and demands, demonstrations, occasional riots, and a growing sense of separatism is common knowledge. Negro pluralism with a rejection of both the long-sought integration with whites and of white leadership, in some cases with an apparent hostility toward "whitey" in any capacity, is a common phenomenon, though it is not shared by all blacks. There is division in Negro ranks, as in others, but there is a common front in the belief that the black man must rebuild his self-image, appreciate his heritage, and assume a place of power in modern life.

The white backlash was inevitable. With white racism and black racism now pitted against each other, what can be done about it? Some suggestions can be made, though with full recognition of their difficulty of achievement.

To follow the sequence of the requirements of justice stated earlier in the chapter, the most needed first step is to recognize that black persons *are persons* of full equality with white persons in native endowment, not an inferior race, and that their equality before God should establish their equality before men. Science has established their biological equality, and such relics of biblically grounded white racism as still survive should be countered by better biblical understanding. The sooner we learn that God "created every race of men of one stock, to inhabit the whole earth's surface" (Acts 17:26, NEB), the better it will be for all.

This recognition of the equality and dignity of all men as persons should lead in several directions. It should lead to the willingness and to an eagerness for meeting in friendly fellowship, both in desegregated schools and in churches. School integration can be commanded by law, that of churches cannot; but the "freedom of choice" in churches makes even more imperative the need to move "with all deliberate speed" from white and black to inter-racial churches. This will not happen rapidly, for since the church is a social institution, strongly influenced by its environment, it is futile to try to wish away the influence of the surrounding culture. Furthermore, since most church have a residential constituency, housing patterns must be changed before there can be any very full integration. Yet

112

neither of these barriers is immovable. Environmental attitudes can be changed, as they have been considerably in recent years, discriminatory housing is being challenged, and a church with sufficient Christian insight can go far toward making its fellowship truly interracial.

Another step that is required is a clearer understanding by whites of why many Negroes, though probably not the majority, are now recoiling from the integration long sought as a goal by both sides. It is tied in with the new mood of ethnocentrism—with the emerging sense of self-identity, racial pride in black achievements, and the desire not only to appreciate one's racial heritage but to fulfill one's racial potentialities. True integration is not the same as assimilation, though for too long integration has meant, often unconsciously, assimilation to the white man's way of doing and thinking. This the black man will permit no longer, and there may need to be a period of separation before integration in the form of a harmonious pluralism can be brought about.[3] Yet one must hasten to say that such pluralism is a far cry from the segregation based on prejudice that has long prevailed, and the mood of withdrawal among Negroes, whether mistaken or not, must not give comfort to white segregationists.

But if such understanding of the roots of black power is required by white persons, the need is reciprocal. The prevalent mood of blacks today is to demand immediate correction of all past and present injustices—no gradualism, no "tokenism." Some in their militancy are ready to use violence, more are not, but there is an almost universal insistence that there be no delay. This mood is understandable but unrealistic. It was indicated earlier that in any move toward the correction of long-standing injustices, progress comes slowly and usually with compromise on both sides as to differing strategies, even with a common goal. To demand "reparations" for three centuries of injustice, or to insist that color rather than competence should determine election to major offices, teaching positions, and other places of leadership, is to court defeat. This is not only because of the white backlash, or the probable failure of the unprepared, but because it is to run counter to the foundations on which all social progress takes place. Furthermore, to condemn white churches, schools, and other groups for tokenism may have a basis when this is a substitute for more inclusive action, but it can also be an evidence of failure to appreciate the fact that slow advance, though under serious difficulties, is still a step toward goals that are being sought.

A basic requirement of justice, we said, is the need to survey the situation, see it from all angles, and make the best possible judgment as to what to do about it. This is needed on both sides of the present chasm. From the standpoint of the white churchman and Christian citizen, it obviously calls for study and discussion of the issues and an attempt to see them objectively, not to reinforce one's prejudices but to get fresh understanding both of evils and their possible remedies. This is a minimum any person can do, and while one may feel helpless to do much more, the study can unexpectedly point out channels of action. Since the racial issue is so largely a personal one, there is seldom an instance where an individual cannot do *something*. Even to change attitudes toward greater racial friendliness means much.

The same principle of the need of knowledge and sound judgment may also be applied to the black thrust toward separation. Is this a wise move? Such leaders as the late Martin Luther King, Roy Wilkins, and Bayard Rustin think not.[4] The advances already won were secured by the joint efforts of white and black; further major advances will come about largely through political and economic action. In politics, in spite of a very valuable extension of voting rights to the Negro, it is mainly white voters who elect the legislators who enact the laws; in economics it is for the most part white employers and the trade unions who can improve the Negro's status. To talk of a separate black state or a Negro party is unrealistic and undercuts the possibilities of improvement which exist. In the colleges a black studies program can be of much service if it is of adequate academic quality and shared with white students who need to know these facts, but not if it is geared toward creating further hostility through unreasonable demands.

Should black studies—and black students—be taught only by black teachers? This points to a deeper question —the legitimate place of white leaders in the black struggle for rights and freedoms long denied. On the one hand, self-determination is a basic right, and it is understandable that those long coerced should wish to demonstrate their independence in strategy as well as in the larger spheres wherein freedom is sought. This should be understood by white sympathizers. On the other hand, repudiation of white assistance not only curtails success but encourages a spirit of divisiveness. When divisiveness becomes hostility, and hostility turns to militancy, and militancy to violence, everybody loses.

White persons who try to act in Christian love should accept without resentment their apparent dismissal from black power leadership, and not obtrude their services. But this does not mean they should stop serving. If what has been thus far said about the self-defeating nature of separatism is true, it places upon white churchmen the greater responsibility for the correction of present forms of injustice through political and economic measures. Not all can do this directly, though many are in administrative and executive positions where they can. The middle-class character of the Protestant churches is often lamented, and they ought to be more supra-class than most of them are. Nevertheless, it is middle-class citizens, and especially the upper middle class, that hold most of the dominant positions of power. And where there is power, there is responsibility.

Even where one is not in a position to exert direct political or economic influence, almost every adult can vote and can express an opinion to his Congressman, which in the aggregate is a weighty influence. Almost every church-member can contribute something toward the Fund for Reconciliation or some other project of racial helpfulness in his denomination. Though what is contributed through the churches may seem "a drop in the bucket" in comparison with the need, it is a precious drop which helps to cement friendship as well as to establish better conditions of human living. And thus through friendship, justice, and service in Christian love, reconciliation moves forward.

Freedom, equality of opportunity, and brotherhood, we said, are the underpinnings of a just society. They are also the foundations of a society in which persons of every race and class might live together, not in identity of pursuits or of opinions, but in mutual respect and good will toward one another. It is our faith that this is the kind of society God desires his human children to have upon the scene where he has placed us. Let us, then, in good faith move as we may in that direction.

The women's liberation movement

We look now at another sphere in which there is a rising tide of protest against injustices of long standing, in some respects similar to, and in others different from, the black power movement. In part this has been precipitated by the demands for black emancipation, though the movement of social forces would probably have brought it into the foreground without this stimulus.

The woman's movement is like the racial one in several features. It is the product of being denied equality of opportunity for centuries—in the case of women, since the dawn of history instead of since the days of slavery. It has resulted in women being regarded as inferior persons and second-class citizens, and often thinking of themselves as such. As more and more women, like the blacks, have become educated and have demonstrated their professional competence, the disparity between their abilities and their opportunities has become the more glaring. Willing to accept this state of affairs no longer, they are speaking out and organizing for action.

Yet there are differences. The major one is that women have long been exalted as wives and mothers, while Negroes were subordinated from every angle. This has the merit of removing women from the status of complete inferiority, while it has had a subtle backlash in making the run-of-the-mill male feel that this is exaltation enough. As a result, men have looked upon women as valued helpers and have expected women to satisfy not only their sexual but personal needs; the male is rare who is willing to see women secure full equality in political, economic, professional, and church relations. Another difference lies in the fact that while the Bible can only by distortion be made to support white racism, there are numerous passages—quite foreign to the spirit and example of Jesus—which subordinate women to their husbands and suggest that positions of authority and power should be held by men only.

What is the result? After centuries of being denied the right to vote, or even to have control over their own property, insurgence arose in the latter half of the nineteenth century, led by such outstanding women as Lucretia Mott,

Elizabeth Cady Stanton, and Susan B. Anthony. In 1920, the Nineteenth Amendment to the Constitution guaranteed women the right to vote. This was followed by the opening up of a good many professions to women, but also by a new lethargy in the "women's rights" movement on the assumption that, with the vote secured, the battle had been won.

The church has been the slowest of all the major institutions to make a place for women in its leadership. Women have, of course, been expected to do "church work" in the form of church suppers, bake sales, and bazaars. In defiance of one part of the injunction in I Timothy 2:12, "I permit no woman to teach or to have authority over men; she is to keep silent," women have done the major part of the Sunday school teaching, but have been given little authority in the church. Women's organizations have been formed in most of the American denominations, which have contributed not only to the local budget but to many other forms of service. It is generally admitted that the ecumenical women's groups, notably the Y.W.C.A. and Church Women United, have often been ahead of the corresponding male bodies in social vision. Yet these contributions have not brought equal status. It is in the ordination of qualified women to the ministry on terms of equality with men, and the election of women to represent the churches in major governing bodies that the barriers have been most rigid.

In recent years these barriers have been challenged both in secular life and in the churches. A number of books have been written which present factual evidence of discrimination and the problems which women encounter as a result.[5] Such challenges have led to the establishment of various organizations of women. The National Woman's Party is seeking an Equal Rights Amendment to the U.S. Constitution, proposed since 1923 but only in 1970 taken seriously enough to be brought to a vote in Congress. NOW

(National Organization of Women) has a major concern for equality in employment, pay, and promotion in the labor market. One organization has the fantastic and satirical title of WITCH (Women's International Terrorist Conspiracy from Hell.) Among most men there seems to be a tendency to treat the matter lightly—whether with alarm I cannot say—but large numbers of women in today's world are very much in earnest about it.

In the churches, doors have opened somewhat, and in a considerable number of the Protestant denominations official barriers to ordination have been removed. Social barriers remain, and few women receive appointments to local parishes, though where these have been secured they for the most part serve effectively. In Catholic circles a number of competent women theologians have emerged, and there are stirrings toward the admission of women to the priesthood, but as yet with no visible results. In membership in church governing bodies and employment in the higher echelons of staff, the number of women grows, though slowly. As in other forms of professional life, salaries are lower for comparable services and promotions to top positions are rarely made.

The movement for the equality of women surfaced at the General Assembly of the National Council of Churches in Detroit, December 1969, along with the demands of blacks and of youth for fuller recognition and opportunity. A women's caucus presented a statement of arresting facts from which it may be useful to cite some excerpts:

Women in this country make 60 cents for every $1.00 a man makes.

Women do not share in the benefits of the fair employment practices laws because those laws do not specify "no discrimination on the basis of sex."

Women often rise in salary only to the point where a man starts.

Women occupy, in great masses, the "household tasks" of industry. They are nurses, not doctors; secretaries, not executives;
researchers, not writers; workers, not managers. . . .

Women almost never occupy decision- or policy-making positions.

Women are almost non-existent in government.

The women present, standing to indicate their agreement
as the statement was read, had also some things to say
about the situation in the churches.

Nowhere is the situation better illustrated than in our male-
dominated and male-oriented churches. The Church, both in its
theology and in its institutional forms, is a reflection of culture.
It has shown no propensity to transcend culture as regards the
status of women, although it knows that it ought. Indeed, the
Church has too often maintained anachronistic attitudes and
practices long after other social institutions have begun to
shift. . . .[6]

Statistics were cited to show the marginal representation of
women in the General Board and General Assembly of the
National Council of Churches, and the disparity of salaries
to those of men where women hold executive positions in
the churches at the national level.

What, then, is to be done about it? As has been suggested
in other connections, a first requirement is to see all persons
as persons, regardless of color, sex, economic status, or
anything else. Not only is "woman's place" in the home—
where it has long been, still is, and doubtless will continue
to be—but woman's place is also in politics, in service
organizations, and in any number of forms of employment.
Granted that women should not neglect their children, most

women have many good years when their presence at home during the day is not required. Granted that men must support families, it is also true that in many households two salaries are needed to meet the rising costs and that there are many women—eight million of them—who are heads of households supporting others than themselves. Granted the complexity of the whole situation, it would appear that employment, compensation, and promotion based on ability rather than sex would more nearly approximate justice than does the present system.

A second requirement is to get the facts and act wisely in the light of them. It was to spread an awareness of these facts that the women's rights advocates of the nineteenth century spoke from many platforms on a trilogy of woman suffrage, temperance, and world peace. The first battle was won; the other two await the combined efforts of men and women. It is to alert their contemporaries to a situation many are unaware of that women's groups today are speaking out.

A third requirement is to secure the enforcement of such laws as now exist. Title VII of the Civil Rights Act of 1964 includes "sex" along with "race, color, religion and national origin" in prohibiting discrimination in employment. But this provision is generally overlooked and almost never enforced.

A fourth requirement is the need to work *with* men, not antagonize them, if the desired fruits are to be attained. For liberty and equality to be established, there must be brotherhood. In the efforts that resulted in the removal of official barriers to women in the ministry of The Methodist Church, in which I am sometimes credited with having a part, I judged it the best strategy to speak when it seemed appropriate to do so, but to trust the men of the church who were sensitive to the issue to carry it to fruition. This might not be the best procedure everywhere, but I know of no situation in which brotherhood is not to be preferred to strife.

Finally, I would counsel women concerned with this vital matter, in the churches and elsewhere, to maintain their femininity, to do the best work they can with the gifts they have, seize such opportunities as become open to them, and not to expect immediate emancipation from age-long prejudice. To clamor for one's rights is less effective than to demonstrate without fanfare that one merits them. As woman suffrage was not won by the more militant suffragettes but by the mind-changing influence of dedicated leaders, millions of nameless women, and the votes of men who saw the justice of it, so further enfranchisement will come about as society is awakened to its need.

Crime and its punishment

I make bold now to speak of an enormous problem of which the concluding pages of this chapter can only touch the fringes. Yet some words upon it are called for because it lies so close to the problem of justice, and hence of reconciliation through justice.

Everyone knows about and is alarmed by the rising tide of crime in our society, and especially in our cities. In many areas it is not safe to be on the streets at night, and bank robberies and other felonies are common occurrences in the daytime. The ultimate crime of murder takes place more often than formerly, and the assassinations of prominent figures in recent years has stirred the public with a sense of horror.

What has caused our crime problem? How is it being dealt with? How could it be corrected? Perhaps some words on each of these questions may yield some pointers in the direction of justice.

First, let it be repeated that the antithesis of justice is

retaliation. When people feel that they must get even for some wrong done them, whether real or imagined, violent emotions are aroused which may lead to violent acts. Other forms of reprisal issue in crimes committed even without physical violence. This is not the only cause of crime, but directly or indirectly, it is responsible for much of it. Furthermore, compounding the tragedy is the fact that much of our penal system is based also on the idea that justice is done when the prisoner is punished in retribution for his offense. Crime must have penalties, but they must be based on other grounds than retaliation if the crime situation is not to be intensified.

Within this general situation, what are the causes of crime? They are manifold, but some are prevalent enough to be identified. One may say that it is all due to sin. In a sense this is true, for self-centeredness and the impulse to anger lurk in all of us and these are at the roots of most crimes. Yet this is not to say that criminals are by nature worse sinners than the rest of us. Barring a few cases of congenital psychic abnormality, most criminals are born as sweet, lovable babies. Perhaps from too little love or too much permissiveness, they grow up thinking that the world is against them or that the world is their free booty to exploit as they can—either or both of these attitudes combined. Some children grow up to be respectable noncriminals, with their sharp business deals, padded expense accounts, evaded income taxes, and hostilities toward families, associates, and other segments of society covered from scrutiny or accepted because "everybody does it." Others less fortunate, lonely, misunderstood, oppressed by poverty, broken families, or the lack of love, drop out of school and then from society as misfits. One may take to drugs and have to steal to get one's "fix," or one may feel that the affluent world owes him a living and rob a bank, or may wish to "get away from it all" and he steals a car. Firearms are plentiful, and when one is caught he shoots, or is shot at, and the result may be homicide.

Another deep imperative to crime is the perfectly natural desire to be noticed, which we all have, but when it is unfulfilled in combination with these other forces, one may escape from anonymity in some startling manner. Dr. Karl Menninger in his eye-opening book, *The Crime of Punishment,* gives this vivid account of how the most famous crime of the century, which changed the currents of history, came about.

Thwarted in repeated efforts to have someone pay attention to his puffed-up insignificance, this nonentity had concealed himself in a warehouse whence he could overlook thousands of his despised fellow citizens. Far below him they were singing hosannas to their radiant, beloved young leader who, despite sneers and smears from a few *other* envious nonentities, had ridden smilingly in an open car through happy throngs of admirers. From his point of vantage far above, the insignificant but ambitious misfit watched intently through a telescope until the right moment.

The little man in the warehouse was no longer anonymous.[7]

I do not know to what extent the prevailing "new morality" contributes to lawbreaking, but its strong emphasis on personal freedom with a repudiation of former taboos and traditions could hardly fail to be a factor. To the extent that it is accompanied by a sense of personal responsibility, such freedom may indicate progress. But immature adolescents and older frustrated misfits can hardly be expected to have a mature sense of responsibility.

What happens to an offender when a crime is committed? In many cases, nothing, and the ability of some to elude arrest emboldens others to take a chance. When captured by the police, soft words and gentleness can hardly be expected, but the coercion used may range from strong-arm methods to blows to a trigger-happy killing. Charges of police brutality are doubtless exaggerated, but enough of it has been seen on television to know that it does exist.

The arrested culprit is taken to jail, where he may or may not be released on bail. I have never been in jail, but dependable reports indicate that they are often dirty, scabrous places where the treatment is based on the assumption that the inmate has forfeited his right to be treated as a person.[8]

Then comes the trial, often after a long delay. Doubtless the jury system was once the best way to establish the suspected person's guilt or innocence. To be tried by one's peers sounds like justice. But is it? The jurors chosen are amateurs, not criminologists or psychiatrists. Furthermore, since they must be persons of so little knowledge of the case as not to have formed an opinion, in a day of rapid and widespread transmission of news, they are apt by this requirement not to be the best informed or most unbiased members of the community. It is not to be wondered at if they are swayed by the lawyer's rhetoric—and by a natural desire to have it over and get home.

And what of the lawyers? A rich defendant can employ a lawyer skilled in all the tricks of getting his client acquitted. The poor man has a lawyer assigned to him, who may be a novice or someone with little interest in his case. The prosecuting attorney is not only an experienced lawyer, but one who has everything to gain in his own prestige and advancement by winning the case. The outcome is often predictable.

The judge is presumably an honest man, more or less unbiased. But his concern is only with the law, not with the prisoner as a person. In sentencing the condemned person, his function is to decide the length of time to be served, not the conditions under which this is to be done.

These conditions vary from prison to prison. But it is certain that a penitentiary is not very apt to make one penitent. Regimentation induces rebellion; idleness makes for mischief toward fellow-prisoners; work, if present, lacks the zest of self-support; lack of normal sex outlets often turns prisons into hotbeds of homosexuality. There is little rehabilitation because there is little reconciliation. The prisoner, when released, is shunned by society, so he turns to his former buddies and before long commits another crime that takes him back to prison again.

This is on the assumption that the offender's penalty is a prison sentence. Sometimes, though less frequently than in the past, the State takes his life in the judicial murder called capital punishment. Most leading jurists are agreed that capital punishment is not a deterrent to crime, and that the danger of electrocuting or sending to the gas chamber an innocent man is too great to justify it. Nevertheless, it continues in a considerable number of states, reinforced by the idea of retribution, not simply with an eye for an eye, but a life for a life.

Within this dismal picture, there are some lights among the shadows. It may, of course, be observed that the situation is worse in the totalitarian states with a drastic curtailment of freedoms, including the basic right of freedom of dissent, and that political prisoners are sometimes made to undergo shocking tortures, if not death, for their convictions. It must also be said that there have been improvements in penal justice within recent years, and we have juvenile courts, correction centers, and systems of probation and parole which have helped to alleviate some of the evils mentioned above. Yet there is much that still needs doing.

The first step, of course, is to prevent crime from occurring. It might not be eliminated but could be much reduced by a greater alertness of the public to the need of loving homes in which there is authority wisely administered, by the curtailment of poverty through adequate employment, by the elimination of racial injustices, by educational and recreational facilities of a creative nature, and in general by a change in social attitudes among the "good" people as well as those who are potential criminals. This requires determined effort by the mind-molding agencies, in which the churches should have a major place. But the needed extension of constructive social agencies takes money also. Were the billions now being spent on the Vietnam War and on frequent journeys to the cold and lifeless moon directed to human need, there could be a great improvement in life on earth, and a radical saving in the high financial cost of crime.

The second step is to detect crime when it occurs, a large proportion of which on all levels now escapes detection, and deal with it in the way best calculated to protect society and rehabilitate the offender. This calls for higher qualifications, further training, and consequently, better pay and higher public esteem for the police. A policeman ought not to be simply a person of sturdy brawn and the usual requirements, and it is not too much to ask that he be trained in the behavioral sciences, especially adolescent psychology, have a usable knowledge of sociology and existing social conditions, and be a creative participant in constructive community efforts. At present a policeman is often required to make a split-second decision on which human lives depend, and he is at the same time relied upon for the security of the public and damned for his brutality. Further training and more discriminate selection might not bring about Utopia, but important steps could be taken toward it.

I shall not attempt to deal with the complex problem of prison reform, save to say that excellent guidelines for it were laid down a hundred years ago. In 1870 some prison administrators met to discuss their problems and drew up a "Statement of Twenty-two Principles," among which are these:

Reformation, not vindictive suffering, should be the purpose of the penal treatment of prisoners.

The prisoner should be made to realize that his destiny is in his own hands.

Prison discipline should be such as to gain the will of the prisoner and conserve his self-respect.

The aim of the prison should be to make industrious free men rather than orderly and obedient prisoners.[9]

The first of these principles, if taken seriously and placed in the context of available scientific knowledge, would take care of all others. Yet before this can come to pass, the public must be alerted to the need of it and both consciences and taxes must be committed to it. If the churches wish to move in the direction of reconciliation through justice— a justice due both from and toward offenders—its gospel of love must replace vengeance and retaliation.

The three problems touched upon in this section are only a few of the problems of justice crying out for solution in our society. I have chosen them for discussion because they impinge upon all of us. The mammoth problems of war and peace, and of poverty and hunger in the midst of affluence, would each require a book for their adequate treatment, and many books have been written upon them. Perhaps enough has been said in outlining some principles of justice through reconciliation for the reader to discern the direction the author takes in thinking upon these problems.

Yet most problems of our society are controversial. Otherwise many of them would have been solved before now and would not be problems. And how is the Christian to conduct himself in the midst of controversy? We shall turn to some guidelines on this issue in the concluding chapter.

7. THE CHRISTIAN
IN CONTROVERSY

What shall we do when controversy breaks out around us, and we find ourselves in the midst of it? Shall we try to "keep the peace" or shall we speak our convictions and thus become personally embroiled in the conflicts of opinion? This is a problem which every Christian, sooner or later, must face. The only alternative is a timid silence which is unworthy of a Christian, and this course, even if followed, is no guarantee of the avoidance of conflict. There *are* times when it is right to be silent—but not through lack of courage or surrender of principle when a real issue is at stake.

The problem

The reason why the problem of controversy is so difficult is that the light we get from the New Testament seems to point in two directions. On the one hand, the obligation of Christian love is central to the teaching of Jesus and to the whole tenor of the gospel message. The supreme duty to love God with all our might finds expression in the duty to love our neighbor as ourselves, and the explicit words of Jesus are, "Blessed are the peacemakers, for they shall be called sons of God." (Matt. 5:9) Add to this such words as those of Paul, "If possible, so far as it depends upon you, live peaceably with all" (Rom. 12:18), and "Love is patient and kind; . . . it is not arrogant or rude" (I Cor. 13:4, 5), and in fact, the entire love chapter, and it would seem our Christian duty to do everything possible to avoid acrimonious conflict.

Yet, on the other hand, Jesus was in conflict throughout his ministry, and died on a cross because he refused to avoid it. He did not hesitate, when the occasion required it, to speak not only forcefully but severely. Whether the sharp words in the twenty-third chapter of Matthew were spoken exactly in this way by Jesus we do not know. Perhaps the gospel writer has made them sound harsher than they would seem to us if we had heard Jesus speak them. Yet there can be no doubt that in regard to the scribes and Pharisees, Jesus "spoke out." Sometimes the controversy took a gentler turn, as when he settled the argument of the disciples as to who was the greatest by setting a child in the midst (Luke 9:46-48), or when he rebuked James and John for wanting to call down fire from heaven to consume the people who would not receive him (Luke 9:53-55). Yet controversy there was, both among those nearest to him and with those whose spirit seemed to him foreign to the way of God. Only before his own accusers was he silent.

Nor did controversy end with the death of Jesus. It appears on almost every page of the book of Acts, and the church was established and spread through Christian witness because the disciples, led by the Holy Spirit, pressed on in spite of it. In Acts 19:23 appears an eloquent understatement, "About that time there arose no little stir concerning the Way." The particular incident at that time was when Demetrius the silversmith, who made silver shrines of the Greek goddess Artemis (called Diana by the Romans) and employed others to work for him, saw the demand decreasing and business being hurt by Paul's preaching against idolatry as he called men to worship in the way of Christ. A riot followed, and Paul might have lost his life then and there if the disciples had not restrained him from going in among the crowd. Riots are nothing new! Shift the names a bit, and the story has a very twentieth-century sound.

This incident at Ephesus was mild in comparison with all that Paul went through as he became embroiled in one controversy after another. In writing to the church at Corinth he gives a vivid and almost breathtaking account of all that he had had to endure in his witness to the gospel. (II Cor. 11:24-28)

Some of these hardships were due to the forces of nature rather than the opposition of persons. Yet there are enough of the latter to indicate that in all probability, the church would never have been established if Peter and Paul and the other disciples had not been able to stand up to controversy.

So, if we are Christians, we must love all persons, even our enemies if we have them, and seek to be peacemakers. At the same time we must stand for the truth and for the right, often at the cost of unpleasant and even dangerous conflict, and serve God in fidelity even if it entails the risk of losing friends, or one's position, or in extreme cases even one's life.

Our problem is, how shall we combine these two ways of acting? Can we combine these two courses in the same situation? Or must we alternate between them? And in any case, how do we keep from being a split personality or an inconsistent Christian?

What follows does not claim to give all the answers. It

is written with the hope of giving some pointers in the direction of an answer.

Some guidelines

In this section we shall look at some directives from the early church which contain words of Christian wisdom that apply equally to every age, including our own. They do not settle all the specific questions for us, but they do indicate the attitudes Christians should have as we seek the solution of particular problems. And without the right attitudes, we shall certainly not find the right deeds to do.

These guidelines will be based, for the most part, on counsel given by Paul in writing to the churches. This does not mean that Paul was infallible, but he dealt wisely with many problems confronting the Christians of his day. His problems, in new forms, are still our problems today.

a. *Have the mind of Christ.* In writing to the Philippians Paul says, "Have this mind among yourselves, which you have in Christ Jesus. . . ." (Phil. 2:5) This injunction stands between counsel enjoining humility and unselfishness and a statement of how Jesus showed these qualities supremely. Elsewhere, Paul raises our familiar question as to how to know the mind of the Lord, that is, the will of God, and he answers it with the assurance, "But we have the mind of Christ." (I Cor. 2:16)

Even though a great book of Christian devotion bears the title, *The Imitation of Christ,* none of us can literally and specifically imitate Christ. Not only did he live in a time, place, and environment different from ours, but he was the Son of God. This leads some people to shy away from using the adjective "Christlike." I remember once being rebuked in an ecumenical meeting when I wanted our report to say that we "must dare to follow Christ's way of life." I was told to say that it was all right to say that we must follow Christ, but to suggest our following his way of life was sheer presumption.

Nevertheless, I still believe that the first requirement of Christian living is to have the mind of Christ; that is, to live with his spirit and message as they come to us through the New Testament. Certainly, our decisions must be made in a different culture and a different kind of world, though the temptations that assail men are not so radically different. Certainly, we can never be as sinless as the Son of God. Yet if we believe in the incarnation, which is central to Christian faith, Jesus so perfectly revealed God that by looking to him as "the pioneer and perfecter of our faith" (Heb. 12:2), we can know God and the tenor of living that God requires of us. In any ticklish problem, we do well to begin by asking ourselves, "If Jesus were here in my place, what would he think? What would he do?" This may not yield the full answer, but it will set our minds and spirits in the right direction.

b. *Speak the truth in love.* In the letter to the Ephesians, we are counseled not to be children, wavering with every kind of idea or form of pressure that comes along. "Rather, speaking the truth in love, we are to grow up in every way into him who is the head, into Christ." (Eph. 4:15) This puts the focus squarely where it belongs—on Christlike love and on the willingness to speak the truth—not in angry denunciation or in querulous faultfinding, but in love.

If we took this seriously and lived by it, it would solve many of our problems. We would be prompted to see the other person's point of view and understand why he thinks as he does, even if we were not led to agree with or excuse him. There is, and doubtless always will be, "the cunning of men" and "their craftiness in deceitful wiles" (Eph. 4:14) to reckon with, and we should not be taken in by these forces. But the way to deal with them is *not* to call bad names, or to impute evil motives simply because of a differing opinion.

A parent, a teacher, or anybody in authority over a child needs to speak firmly, and at times sharply. To rebuke wrongdoing is as necessary as to praise right doing. But to do this in anger or an emotional outburst is bad both for the speaker and the one spoken to, and violence, whether of speech or action, begets more violence. This is just as true on the adult level. Long before the coming of Jesus, a bit of homely wisdom was included in the book of Proverbs,

> A soft answer turns away wrath,
> but a harsh word stirs up anger (Prov. 15:1)

With the coming of Jesus and the birth of the church, the spirit of love includes but transcends this common sense wisdom. To speak the truth in love would be *right,* regardless of results. The way of love does not always "work" in the sense of converting the opponent or bringing about social harmony. Yet nothing else in the long run is so effective. It is significant that the passage about growing into Christian maturity through speaking the truth in love continues on the note of unity within the Body of Christ.

c. *Be aglow with the Spirit.* The need to put love at the center of our acting and to do this at the leading of the Holy Spirit are brought together in a memorable capsule in Paul's letter of counsel to the church at Rome. In the middle of the twelfth chapter he writes:

Let love be genuine; hate what is evil, hold fast to what is good; love one another with brotherly affection; outdo one another in showing honor. Never flag in zeal, be aglow with the Spirit, serve the Lord. Rejoice in your hope, be patient in tribulation, be constant in prayer. (Rom. 12:9-12)

What does it mean to be "constant in prayer"? Certainly it does not mean to be addressing God at every moment, whether in spoken words or silent meditation. There are those who enter cloisters to withdraw from the world and spend many hours each day in prayer, but for most of us God has work to do within the world, even in the world of controversy and conflicting opinions. To be constant in prayer is to live and do our work in responsiveness to God's Spirit.

We need to be responsive to the Spirit, or as Paul puts it vividly, to "be aglow with the Spirit" in situations both of harmony and of controversy. As we need it in the former to keep from getting too self-satisfied, we need it in the latter to give us guidance and strength when the going gets rough. The fourth creed in the United Methodist ritual, written many years ago by Bishop Herbert Welch and sometimes called the Korean Creed, affirms, "We believe in the Holy Spirit, God present with us for guidance, for comfort and for strength." We believe this with our minds, but do we always with our hearts?

In any situation where the answer is not clear, we ought certainly to pray, and to pray with the willingness to follow whatever light may come from God. Along with this, we ought to look at the entire situation as broadly and objectively as possible, and to use our best thinking to try to determine which course would contribute to the greatest good of everyone involved. Not only should we have special and earnest times of prayer about the issue, but if the persons with whom we are in controversy are also Christians, we ought to try to pray together about our differences. The Quakers have a practice, when "the sense of the meeting" is not clear because of differing views, of entering into a period of silence. Within the silence it usually follows that the Holy Spirit speaks in such a way that when human speaking is resumed, there is agreement.

At the conclusion of the beatitudes, as Luke states them, we find these words, "But I say to you that hear, Love your enemies, do good to those who hate you, bless those who curse you, pray for those who abuse you." (Luke 6:27,28) This difficult injunction we shall certainly not live up to without the help of the Holy Spirit. And as we look further at the last clause, we see that it is important to pray *for* those who hurt us, not *at* them. The spirit of this injunction is violated if, with a self-pitying and self-righteous sting in the words, we ask the Lord to make our opponent stop bothering us.

d. *Test everything; hold fast what is good.* Again we find the directives of the gospel tied together in a compact unity, for in Paul's first letter to the Thessalonians he writes, "Do not quench the Spirit, do not despise prophesying, but test everything; hold fast what is good, abstain from every form of evil." (I Thess. 5: 19-22). This appears in the context of other wise counsel about respecting authority, living peaceably, encouraging the fainthearted, being patiently helpful, doing good to one another instead of trying to get even for an injury.

What does it mean to "test everything"? It means, in the first place, to get the facts. A great deal of trouble is caused by emotions being aroused by false statements that are believed to be true without being examined. Every political campaign provides examples. Unfortunately, many believe charges of Communist infiltration into the Protestant churches and the National Council of Churches which are completely false. In a similar vein, detractors accuse the translators of the Revised Standard Version of distorting the Bible. To test everything means to find out the facts, and not jump to conclusions on the basis of misinformation.

To test everything means, further, that we should use our minds to see the whole situation, not being carried away by one angle of it. Counselors cannot do our thinking for us, but they can often help us to see the larger picture. It is important that in any decision we should foresee the consequences as clearly as possible and try with God's help to decide what will be of the greatest service to all who are affected by the decision. A necessary aspect of this is to judge how it will affect our own future serving, not our comfort or income or easy living or pleasure, but our *serving*.

For such a decision we need all the light we can get from the Christian gospel. But we need also some contemporary light on contemporary problems, and this may be why Paul says in the passage in Thessalonians, "Do not despise prophesying." If we remember that the prophets were persons of deep conviction who spoke for God to the people, we can find this note in prophetic preaching today. Not all preaching today is prophetic, but our intuitions will generally tell us when it is! Again, the resolutions passed by the governing bodies of the churches may fall short of authentic Christian wisdom, but they are generally the result of careful Christian thought and ought to be considered seriously as we attempt to "test everything, hold fast what is good."

e. *All things are not expedient.* Again Paul wrote to the Corinthian church, "All things are lawful unto me, but all things are not expedient." (I Cor. 6:12 KJV) The Revised Standard Version renders it, "Not all things are helpful." Paul apparently was urging the people to whom he was writing to have a sense of the fitness of things, and therefore not to exercise *all* the freedom they could. Though Paul was speaking of freedom in Christ from the old Mosaic law, the principle holds true in many circumstances today.

It is a Christian duty not to let our zeal outrun our wisdom, but to keep them together. I suspect this was what Jesus meant when he told his disciples he was sending them out as sheep in the midst of wolves, so they should be "wise as serpents and innocent as doves." (Matt. 10:16)

In short, strategy matters. If we are trying to accomplish something in the Lord's work, we should not defeat our ends by acting foolishly. We should stick by our principles, but this does not mean throwing caution and restraint to the winds. We should never compromise our goals, but we may reach them faster if we do not try to get there too fast. "Gradualism" ought never to be a substitute for action or a cover for cowardice, but in many circumstances it is the part of Christian wisdom to be clearsighted about what can be accomplished and not expect everything to be done at once.

An example or two may make this clearer. One may be conscientiously a Christian pacifist, but if this is one's only approach to the problem of peace and war, he will do less for the cause of peace than if he works for peace and world order side by side with other Christians who are not pacifists. One may believe that there ought to be full and complete equality between the races, including intermarriage, but in the present state of racial tensions intermarriage may not be the best approach to race equality. Much as we deplore the anti-Communist hysteria which brands prophetic Christian social action as Communist-inspired, we had better not sign statements, however innocent sounding, put out by Communists, or support meetings they sponsor, or be taken in by their propaganda.

f. *Do not be conformed to this world.* In the twelfth chapter of Romans, a compendium of good counsel for Christians, Paul writes, "Do not be conformed to this world

139

but be transformed by the renewal of your mind, that you may prove what is the will of God, what is good and acceptable and perfect." (Rom. 12:2) Here he hits us right between the eyes! It would be so much easier to be a Christian and live by "the mind of Christ" if the pulls of our society were not so strong in the other direction! Yet they *are* strong and always have been, and Christians must live in the midst of them. If they were not so strong, there would probably be no need of writing a chapter about "The Christian in Controversy."

In principle Paul gives the answer: "Be transformed by the renewal of your mind." The church needs renewal; so do we all. We need daily renewal through prayer and the message God has for us in the Bible; through careful thought on the problems of society as well as on our own; through worship and Christian fellowship in the church; through acting for God by the light we have.

In the seventh chapter of John there is recorded an incident which can help us in our time, though its setting is long ago. The people could not make up their minds whether to listen to Jesus and "there was much muttering about him among the people." (John 7:12) Jesus placed his authority on firm ground when he told the people that if they were willing to do God's will, they would know whether his teaching was from God. We must not oversimplify this to suppose that sincerity in doing God's will can settle all our problems. Yet it is a prime requisite for being "transformed by the renewal of your mind" instead of conforming to the opinions and mutterings of the people about us. It makes the focus right and then the whole picture becomes much clearer.

g. *We must obey God rather than men.* With this general principle all Christians would agree. Everything we have said thus far implies it. But what if our consciences lead us to clash with those in authority over us? In short, to defy an edict or to break a law?

There is precedent for this in Acts, when Peter found himself in a controversy which prompted him to say, "We must obey God rather than men." (Acts 5:29.) Read the story as it is found in the fifth chapter of Acts, beginning at the twelfth verse, and note in it not only Peter's courage but also Gamaliel's wise advice. The story comes to a resounding climax in the apostles' continuing to do exactly what they had been forbidden to do, "rejoicing that they were counted worthy to suffer dishoner for the name." (v. 41).

This is serious. Such steps ought never to be taken lightly, or without deep prayer and a full counting of the cost. One must be *very sure* that the edict or the law one disobeys is contrary to the will of God as we discern it from the message and spirit of Jesus, rather than merely its being annoying or displeasing to us. Yet there come times, as in the case of the German Christians who defied Hitler, when a higher loyalty must prevail. Although Dietrich Bonhoeffer and Martin Niemoller are the most famous of those who took this stand, there were others, and we spontaneously admire their courage. In this country the issue has come most into focus over the refusal to participate in or give support to a war that is regarded by many as unjust, immoral, and contrary to the will of God as discerned through the teachings of Jesus. The issue will doubtless remain a controversial one, and the problem of how to deal with it calls into play all the guidelines previously stated in this chapter.

This brings to a close the discussion in this book of the ministry of reconciliation. Yet the doing remains! John Drinkwater spoke words of great truth when he wrote these lines:

Knowledge we ask not—knowledge thou has lent,
But, Lord, the will—there lies our deepest need,
Give us to build above the deep intent
    The deed, the deed.[1]

Yet one who will doubtless be quoted long after Drink-water has been forgotten summed it up for us in these words, "Therefore, if any one is in Christ, he is a new creation; the old has passed away, behold, the new has come. All this is from God, who through Christ reconciled us to himself and gave us the ministry of reconciliation." With so high a mandate, can we fail to act?

NOTES

1. WHAT IS RECONCILIATION?

1. (New York: Sheed and Ward, 1969.)
2. *Ibid.*, p. 6.
3. See *Moral Man and Immoral Society: A Study in Ethics and Politics.* (New York: Scribner's, 1932).
4. *Christianity and Crisis,* Sept. 16, 1969, p. 242.

2. RECONCILIATION IN THE OLD TESTAMENT

1. Article on "Atonement" by C. L. Mitton, Vol. A-D, p. 310.
2. A more extended presentation and analysis of these codes may be found in my book, *The Sources of Western Morality* (New York: Scribners, 1954), chapters 5 and 6.

3. RECONCILIATION IN THE NEW TESTAMENT

1. The Synoptic Gospels, so called from the Greek which means "seeing with one view," are Matthew, Mark and Luke. There is much similarity in their presentation of the life and ministry of Jesus. They are generally regarded as being more historically reliable than John, which was written later from a quite different point of view.
2. I am aware that the authorship of Ephesians is in dispute, and for this reason am quoting only guardedly from this letter. Personally, I believe that the evidence for the Pauline authorship is at least as strong as that against it.

4. RECONCILIATION IN THE INDIVIDUAL PERSON

1. See "Three Damoclean Swords" by J. Robert Nelson in *The Christian Century* of January 21, 1970, for the interaction of theologians and scientists on these issues.
2. In Fromm's terminology, "productiveness" is the key to mentally healthy and happy living and to sound morality. Since there are many kinds of productivity, including that of the "marketing orientation" which Fromm disparages, this term seems too ambiguous.
3. For an excellent analysis of these terms and their significance in the contemporary setting, see Ian G. Barbour, *Issues in Science and Religion* (Englewood Cliffs, N.J.: Prentice-Hall, 1966), Chapter XI entitled "Life and Mind."
4. See *Man for Himself,* pp. 231-37 for an elaboration of this view.
5. John B. Cobb, Jr., *God and the World* (Philadelphia: Westminster Press, 1969), p. 65.
6. For a fuller statement the reader is referred to the author's *The Dark Night of the Soul* (Nashville: Abingdon Press, 1945; paperback, 1968), especially to Chapter X. While it is not a recent book, the selected bibliography was brought up to date for the paperback edition.
7. *Science and the Modern World* (New York: Macmillan, 1931), p. 275.
8. *The Dark Night of the Soul,* p. 179.
9. *Reality in Worship* (New York: Macmillan, 1925), p. 30.
10. Miguel de Unamuno in *The Tragic Sense of Life.* Excerpt in *The Nature of Man* edited by Erich Fromm and Ramón Xirau (New York: Macmillan, 1968), p. 268.

5. RECONCILIATION THROUGH FRIENDSHIP

1. If the reader is interested, he will find an account of these relations in my *Grace Abounding* (Nashville: Abingdon Press, 1969), pp. 30-44.
2. *The Ways of Friendship,* pp. 41-43.
3. *I-Thou* (New York: Scribner's, 1937, 1958), p. 11. This is the main theme of this celebrated and influential book.

4. Those readers who have seen *A Special Way of Victory* by Dorothea Waitzmann (Richmond: John Knox Press, 1964) which I edited, may be interested to know that Miss Waitzmann and I have never met in person, though we have developed over the years a firm and mutually rewarding friendship through correspondence. The book is the story of one who has been handicapped by cerebral palsy from birth and of the remarkable adjustment to life she has made.

5. *The Ways of Friendship,* p. 15.

6. RECONCILIATION THROUGH JUSTICE

1. Emil Brunner, *Justice and the Social Order* (New York: Harper, 1945), pp. 19-20.

2. *Politics,* Book IV, section 1291b. Richard McKeon, ed., *The Basic Works of Aristotle* (New York: Random House, 1941), p. 212.

3. This is the conclusion of Joseph C. Hough, Jr., in his excellent *Black Power and White Protestants* (New York: Oxford University Press, 1968).

4. For an excellent statement of the wider implications of the case against Negro separatism by an outstanding Negro leader, see Bayard Rustin, "The Failure of Black Separatism," in *Harper's Magazine,* January, 1970.

5. Among the most influential of these books are *American Women: The Changing Image* (Boston: Beacon Press, 1962) by eleven distinguished women; *The Feminine Mystique* (New York: Norton, 1963) by Betty Friedan; *The Church and the Second Sex* (New York: Harper, 1968) by Mary Daly. Of a more official nature is *American Women: Report of the President's Commission on the Status of Women, 1963,* the Commission having been appointed by President Kennedy. President Nixon has appointed a similar Commission, which has endorsed the Equal Rights Amendment.

6. Quotations from the statement are taken from *The Church Woman,* March, 1970, pp. 18-19.

7. (New York: The Viking Press), 1966, 1968, p. 27.

8. It may be recalled that when Karl Barth visited America, he asked to see some jails and was shocked by what he found.
9. Menninger, *The Crime of Punishment,* p. 219.

7. THE CHRISTIAN IN CONTROVERSY

1. John Drinkwater, *Poems* (Boston: Houghton Mifflin, 1919). Used by permission.

QUESTIONS
FOR DISCUSSION

Chapter 1

1. What does the word reconciliation mean to you?
2. Make a comprehensive list of contemporary situations in which you think reconciliation is greatly needed.
3. Select one or more of these situations for group discussion and consider together: (1) the main factors that have caused the situation, (2) what needs to be done about it, (3) how the churches can help, (4) what *you* can do.
4. From your church periodical or other sources, describe a significant project of reconciliation in which your denomination is engaged.
5. What is your local church doing now to further the ministry of reconciliation? What more should it be doing?

Chapter 2

1. How is atonement related in its meaning to reconciliation?
2. How does expiation differ from propitiation in reference to human sin?
3. Look up the biblical references cited in reference to ritualistic acts of atonement. What values and shortcomings did these Old Testament practices have?

4. It is sometimes said that the worship of the churches today is as empty of meaning as the prophets charged against the rituals of their time. Do you agree?

5. Cite several passages from the Psalms, other than those in the text, which bear on the experience of reconciliation. What is the connection?

6. Learn what you can of the covenant concept in the Old Testament. What is its relationship to reconciliation and to Hebrew history as a whole?

7. Point out provisions in Israel's moral codes that have relevance to the present and show how they apply.

8. Look up the references to peace cited in the text and indicate how they apply to our current situation.

Chapter 3

1. Christians have always thought of Jesus as "Christ the Lord." What more does this mean than simply to say "Jesus"?

2. How did Paul's own experience affect his theology?

3. The author of the text speaks of two mistakes made by Paul with important results for the future. Do you agree or not?

4. What were the great positive notes in Paul's message? Indicate why and how each of these was important.

5. What is the theological difference between sin and sins? How is each of these meanings related to reconciliation?

6. Indicate particular ways in which the ministry and the teaching of Jesus give us directives for reconciliation today in spite of the differences between his world and ours. If you think this is not possible, show why.

7. "We need to see the life, the message, the death and the resurrection of Jesus all as part of one supreme event

in human history." Why is each element essential to all
the others?

8. Show how the early church dealt with conflict as this
   is indicated in the book of Acts and the Letters. Cite
   illustrative passages.

Chapter 4

1. The text lists numerous sources of anxiety in our time.
   Do you agreee with those listed? Would you add others?
2. What is *right* with modern life?
3. With regard to each of the distinctive notes in the Christian understanding of man, what difference does it make
   in your own living?
4. What difference do they, or should they, make in the
   mission of the church?
5. If you should feel a need for counseling, what sort of
   equipment in personal qualities, professional skills, and
   basic beliefs would you wish to find in your counselor?
6. Group therapy and sensitivity training are much in vogue
   today. With what affirmative accents and/or safeguards
   should they be used in the churches?
7. Evaluate the guidelines at the end of *Reconciliation in
   psychotherapy and religion* as to their importance and
   how best to use them.
8. What is evangelism? What kinds are most needed in the
   churches today?

Chapter 5

1. How would you define friendship? How is it related to
   reconciliation?
2. What kinds of attitudes and procedures in individuals
   encourage it? Thwart it?
3. What social conditions around you tend to have these

effects? And how can those that thwart friendship be changed?

4. What more must be done in society as a whole to bridge present barriers of race, economic and social status, and religion?

5. Make a list of the most prevalent causes of disharmony in families. What steps need to be taken in each of these situations to reduce the danger of tension and conflict?

6. What should the churches be doing to promote better family life?

7. What constructive services can you report which are being done by the young people of today?

8. If there are disruptive tensions in your local church, work with other church members to make a constructive analysis of the situation. But take care not to deepen hostilities by being too judgmental!

Chapter 6

1. One of the most difficult problems of human relations is to find a combination of freedom and restraint which will avoid both anarchy and oppression. How does this apply to the present social situation?

2. Some hold that the teachings of Jesus give no direction for current social problems because our times are so different from his. Do you agree?

3. What is your view of the relationship of justice to love? Apply this to punishment in the home and in society as a whole.

4. Try to imagine yourself on the other side of the present color chasm. What might you then say in defense of that point of view?

5. From the standpoint of your own race, what do you regard as the most desirable steps to take to advance reconciliation with justice?

6. There are some indications that sex discrimination is more deeply rooted and harder to overcome than racial discrimination. What is your opinion?

7. Why has the church been slower than other social institutions to accept women in its professional leadership?

8. Many Protestant churches now officially permit the ordination of women, but there are few women ministers. What do you think should be done about it?

9. If penalties for crime ought not to be based on retaliation, what should be the foundations?

10. What reforms in our present judicial and penal systems do you advocate?

11. What ought the churches to do about them?

Chapter 7

1. Cite an instance in which a Christian should try to be a peacemaker and another in which he ought to speak out even at the risk of conflict. What makes the difference?

2. Read Acts 19:23-41. How does this incident resemble what happens today?

3. How do we acquire "the mind of Christ"?

4. Some poeple believe violence works where love does not. What do you think?

5. What are the values and limits of prayer in making moral decisions?

6. What does it mean to love God "with all your mind" (Matt. 22:37)?

7. Is civil disobedience ever justified? If so, under what circumstances?

8. What new insights have you acquired in this study of the ministry of reconciliation? In what ways do you hope to have these affect your Christian living?

151

SELECTED BIBLIOGRAPHY

Chapter 1

Bianchi, Eugene C., *Reconciliation—The Function of the Church* New York: Sheed & Ward, 1969. Written by a Roman Catholic, applicable to all churches.

Come, Arnold B., *Agents of Reconciliation* Philadelphia: Westminster Press, 1960, 1964. Laymen in the reconciling mission of the church.

Nelson, John Oliver, *Dare to Reconcile: Seven Settings for Creating Community* New York: Friendship Press, 1969. Surveys conflict situations with suggestions for reconciliation.

Rutenber, C. G., *Reconciling Gospel* Nashville: Broadman Press, 1969. As its title indicates.

Wentz, Frederick K., *Set Free for Others* New York: Friendship Press, 1969. Deals with both inner and social alienation and reconciliation.

Chapters 2, 3

The bibliography for these two chapters is combined because many of the books deal with both the Old and New Testaments. In others, titles show these differentiations.

Baab, Otto J., *The Theology of the Old Testament* Nashville: Abingdon Press, 1959. Especially good on Old Testament ideas of sin and salvation.

DeWolf, L. Harold, *The Enduring Message of the Bible* New York: Harper, 1960. Admirable for lay readers.

Fosdick, H. E., *A Guide to Understanding the Bible* New York: Harper, 1938. Does not grow stale with time.

Harkness, Georgia, *Christian Ethics* Nashville: Abindgdon Press 1957, Part I. Historical and analytical.

Knox, John, *On the Meaning of Christ* New York: Scribner's, 1947. None better on the Christ event.

———, *The Death of Christ* Nashville: Abingdon Press, 1958. The Cross in New Testament history and faith.

Lillie, William, *Studies in New Testament Ethics* Philadelphia: Westminster Press, 1961, 1963. Both scholarly and practical.

Manson, T. W., *Ethics and the Gospel* New York: Scribner's, 1960. Both Old and New Testament origins of Christian ethics.

Smith, J. M. Powis, *The Moral Life of the Hebrews* Chicago: University of Chicago Press, 1923. Old, but unsurpassed in its field.

Taylor, Vincent, *The Atonement in New Testament Teaching* London: Epworth Press, 1940, 1945. A classic treatment of its theme.

Whale, J. S., *Victor and Victim: The Christian Doctrine of Redemption.* Cambridge: The University Press, 1960. The Cross in the life, worship and doctrine of the Church.

Wolf, William J., *No Cross, No Crown* New York: Doubleday, 1957. The atonement from various perspectives, biblical, theological, experiential.

Different in structure and purpose from any of the above is *The Interpreter's Dictionary of the Bible* Nashville: Abingdon Press, 1962. A definitive and scholarly treatment of many Biblical themes in four volumes. See especially "Atonement," Vol. A-D, pp. 309-13; "Covenant," Vol. A-D, pp. 714-23; "Forgiveness," Vol. E-J pp. 314-19; "Reconciliation," Vol. R-Z, pp. 16-17.

Chapter 4

Clinebell, Howard J., Jr., *Mental Health Through Christian Community* Nashville: Abingdon Press, 1965. Many aspects of the local church's ministry of growth and healing.

Fromm, Erich, *Man for Himself* New York: Holt, Rinehart & Winston, 1947. A basic book on psychotherapy.

———, *Psychoanalysis and Religion* New Haven: Yale University Press, 1950. How religion is related to mental health, sometimes adversely.

Grimes, Howard, *The Church Redemptive* Nashville: Abingdon Press, 1958. Inner reconciliation through worship and the on-going life of the church.

Maves, Paul B., ed., *The Church and Mental Health* New York: Scribner's, 1953. On potential forms of service in the church.

May, Rollo, *Love and Will* New York: W. W. Norton, 1969. One of the most important books in its field.

Menninger, Karl A. *Man Against Himself* New York: Harcourt, Brace & World, 1956. Man's conflicts as viewed by a famous psychologist.

Niebuhr, Reinhold, *The Nature and Destiny of Man,* Vol. I New York: Scribner's, 1941. A classic, somewhat difficult but rewarding.

Outler, Albert C., *Psychotherapy and the Christian Message* New York: Harper, 1954. Excellent in both theology and psychology.

Roberts, David E., *Psychotherapy and a Christian View of Man* New York: Association Press, 1950. Same comment as on Outler.

Chapter 5

Ackerman, Nathan W., *The Psychodynamics of Family Life* New York: Basic Books, 1958. Better mental health through better family life.

Baruch, Dorothy W., *How to Live With Your Teenager* New York: McGraw-Hill, 1953. What many parents need to know.

Duvall, Evelyn and Reuben Hill, *When Your Marry* New York: Association Press, 1953, 1962. Good counsel for both young people and their elders.

Fromm, Erich, *The Art of Loving,* New York: Harper, 1956. What we all need to have.

Howe, Reuel, *The Creative Years* New York: Seabury Press, 1958. How to make them more creative.

Lepp, Ignace, *The Ways of Friendship* New York: Macmillan, 1966. Very helpful.

Mace, David R. *Success in Marriage* Nashville: Abingdon Press, 1958. Wise counsel.

Popenoe, Paul, *Marriage Is What You Make It* New York: Macmillan, 1952. Practical wisdom from an expert.

See chapter seven for references on relations in churches.

Chapter 6

No references are given on justice because almost every book on social ethics deals with this theme.

ON RACE AND BLACK POWER

Cone, James H. *Black Theology and Black Power* New York: Seabury Press, 1969. A very arresting presentation of the black point of view.

Haselden, Kyle, *The Racial Problem in Christian Perspective* New York: Harper, 1959. A penetrating and well-balanced statement.

Hough, Joseph C. Jr., *Black Power and White Protestants* New York: Oxford University Press, 1968. A white Protestant explains the black position.

Maston, T. B., *The Bible and Race,* Nashville: Broadman Press, 1959. Corrects common errors.

ON THE WOMEN'S LIBERATION MOVEMENT

Culver, Elsie Thomas, *Women in the World of Religion* Garden City, N.Y.: Doubleday, & Co., 1967. A historical survey from early times to the present.

Gibson, Elsie, *When the Minister is a Woman* New York: Holt, Reinhart & Winston, 1970. Presents the results of research and evaluates the issues.

For other references see footnote on page 00.

ON CRIME AND PUNISHMENT

Menninger, Karl, *The Crime of Punishment* New York: The Viking Press, 1968. Shows clearly how wrong we are in modes of dealing with offenders.

Rowland, Stanley J., Jr., *Ethics, Crime and Redemption* Philadelphia: Westminster Press, 1963. What the churches might be doing about it.

Chapter 7

Abbey, Merrill R., *Preaching to the Contemporary Mind* Nashville: Abingdon Press, 1963. How to achieve a meeting of minds.

King, Martin Luther, Jr., *Strength to Love* New York: Harper, 1963. Sermons mainly on social issues by one who had this strength.

Rasmussen, Albert T., *Christian Social Ethics* Englewood Cliffs, N.J.: Prentice-Hall, 1956. Valuable suggestions on exerting Christian influence.

Seifert, Harvey J., and Clinebell, Howard J., Jr., *Personal Growth and Social Change* Philadelphia: Westminster Press, 1969. A guide for ministers and laymen as agents of change.

INDEX